Carson's

Carson's

THE HISTORY OF A
CHICAGO SHOPPING LANDMARK

GAYLE SOUCEK

Charleston   London

THE
History
PRESS

Published by The History Press
Charleston, SC 29403
www.historypress.net

Copyright © 2013 by Gayle Soucek
All rights reserved

Back cover, middle: Courtesy of the Art Institute of Chicago.
Unless otherwise noted, all pictures from the author's collection.

First published 2013

Manufactured in the United States

ISBN 978.1.60949.734.7

Library of Congress CIP data applied for.

Those we love don't go away; they walk beside us every day.
Unseen, unheard, but always near; still loved, still missed and very dear.
—anonymous

This book is dedicated to the memories of Martha Ward Miller
and Lavergne M. Soucek

CONTENTS

Chicago's Iconic State Street

C hicago has always been known for its magnificent department stores offering an emporium of goods and assisted salesperson service, or clerks, along with an unprecedented and creative means to promote, market and sell products within the given establishment. This was often partnered with a beautiful, open-air, light-filled and spacious architectural environment to showcase products and an unparalleled sense of arrival to these institutions and buildings as a destination. The unique and all-encompassing marketing approach to these department stores, where a customer could spend a full day shopping, dining and relaxing, has been duplicated on many levels around the globe, but many attribute the origins, or the perfection of the concept, "all under one roof" and on a grand scale, to the merchants and "merchant princes" of State Street and the grand vision of a retailing mecca.

Democratic in its approach and outreach to all people, open and free to anyone willing to walk through and at one time creating a path from one store to another, like a continuous arcade, for nearly a mile down the east side of State Street from Randolph to Congress Parkway, was a variety of stores and goods ranging from the exotic to the most mundane. These department stores and large specialty retailers, each with its own vision, personality and spirit, were long viewed by many shoppers as an extension of public institutions and, over time, evolved into full-service department and specialty stores. Often marketed with a cultural bent of events and exhibits to entice shoppers, the retailers further blurred the definition between museum, cultural institution and retailing showcase and reflected select parts and highlights of Chicago and other cities and countries. One institution in particular proclaimed that its edifice and store was essentially all Chicago in many ways, part of a 1980s campaign by Marshall Field and Company as the institution neared its 130th birthday: "Marshall Field's is Chicago." This was a motto that followed the store for many years, and ironically, many people may have agreed that the large retailer did represent the city and its history in so many different ways.

For more than 150 years, State Street, also known as the "Great Street" for its variety of shopping and entertainment, density of shoppers and even the brightness of its lights and signage, was the epicenter of retailing and shopping in Chicago. This destination district, anchoring Chicago's downtown, was once lined with theaters, dating back to vaudeville and talkies to full movie theaters, with their brilliant marquees, top entertainment, luxury hotels—some of the world's largest or tallest at the time of their construction—and legendary restaurants located on the street or within a short distance away.

Tall buildings lined with businesses for jewelry, clothes, dentist and medical offices and small enterprises prevailed between the larger retailers, from the Masonic Temple (later known as the Capitol Building)—the world's tallest in the 1890s with its twenty-two-story atrium—to the Reliance Building, Steven's Building, Columbus Memorial Building, Marshall Field Annex and Venetian Building, noted among many. These edifices composed both State Street and nearby adjoining streets and were located within late nineteenth- and early twentieth-century office buildings.

The bright lights and legends of State Street radiated throughout the Loop or central business district, and most all transit systems, including the elevated "L," subway, cable car, streetcar and bus lines, linked to this popular shopping mecca. It was the epitome of shopping, culture and entertainment, a city's life and breath. While Chicago's many neighborhoods and ethnic enclaves had many smaller stores and even branch stores of those downtown nameplates, and while Michigan Avenue had its expensive specialty stores, nothing rivaled State Street in its appeal, volume of shoppers, expansive sales reports and liveliness. It was a story of over-saturating a street with as many stores as possible to attract the largest audience, and it most likely began with the vision of a few retailers, landholders and investors, continuing from the 1870s to the present day. The popular 1940s radio jingle "What do you want? And what do you want to pay? State Street has it every day!" sums up the vast array of goods offered to the consumer.

Marshall Field and Company was perhaps the grande dame, with a store occupying a full city block, thirteen stories tall and bounded by State, Randolph, Wabash and Washington Streets. Its separate Men's Store and Annex Building were located across Washington Street and occupied a quarter of a city block and the first seven floors of the 25 East Washington Street, with another volume of office floors above. The Marshall Field and Company store sold everything from elaborate and designer clothes in the 28 Shop, handmade and antique furnishings, English antique silver dating to the 1700s and art to hardware, bolts of fabrics and sporting goods, including its own special house labels and prepared food products. These food items often matched popular menu entrées served in its seven restaurants, most located on the seventh floor and "Budget Floor" or basement of the State Street flagship. These items ranged from a small frozen whole piglet, with an apple in its mouth, to the famous Chicken Pot Pie and items from each of the restaurants, mostly from the more formal and exclusive Walnut Room (originally known as the South Grill). However, entrées from the English Room, Narcissus Room (originally known as the North Grill), the Veranda, the Buffet (a cafeteria) and the Bowl & Roll were also part of the selection. Most customers had a favorite restaurant in the store that they had certain affections toward and became a routine at each visit, creating a friendly rivalry between the formal Walnut Room and the fish and chips served in the more casual English Room. The Buffet or cafeteria sold all the items on the separate menus offered in each restaurant, just in case the lines to be seated were long, which was often the case. Field's also had a full-service bakery, which reflected many dessert items from the restaurants and more.

Among the other top-tier stores were Carson Pirie Scott; Chas A. Stevens, a women's store on State Street extending to Wabash Avenue; Mandel Brothers, fronting State Street to Wabash Avenue, known after 1960 as Wieboldt's, which also had many neighborhood stores; and Netcher's Boston Store at State and Madison (now the home of the newer Sears Store, extending to Dearborn and one of the few remaining large retail stores on the west side of State Street). Extending south were Bond's; Baskin; Henry C. Lytton (also known as "Lytton's" and "The Hub"); Goldblatt Bros. (originally the Rothschild Store and the Davis Store, a moderate-priced branch of the Marshall Field store); The Fair at State and Adams (later known as Montgomery Ward); Maurice Rothschild at the southwest corner of State and Jackson; and, at the southern terminus of State Street, the Sears Roebuck (formerly known as Siegel & Cooper and constructed within the Leiter II Building by architect William LeBaron Jenney, father of the skyscraper) store. Of the topmost bracket were Marshall Field and Carson's, perhaps from the beginning, much like the New York rivals Macy's and Gimbels, across 34th Street from each other, with the famous saying "Does Macy's tell Gimbels?"

Carson's, known officially as Carson Pirie Scott and Company, always had high-quality standards and a contemporary edge and was fresh, stylish and vogue, in sharp contrast to the more refined, restrained and sometimes stuffy formality of Marshall Field, also commonly known as simply "Field's."

Carson Pirie Scott and Company traced its early history to downstate Illinois, in Amboy, and small cities before arriving in 186 on Chicago's Lake Street, a precursor to State Street in the period from 1850 to 1880. The Chicago store was operated by Andrew MacLeish, a Scotsman, in partnership with Samuel Carson, John T. Pirie and later joined by the Scott brothers. MacLeish fostered the wholesale and dry goods business (later referred to as retail). This led to focusing many efforts on the Chicago store and, after the Great Chicago Fire of 1871, on State Street and the Chicago Loop.

In 1895, Carson Pirie Scott and Company moved into the lower floor of the Reliance Building, by architect D.H. Burnham & Company, with Charles Atwood as designer (now known as the Hotel Burnham and the Atwood Cafe). Expansion on this site was considered to be growing westward into the Portland Block, an 1870s building by William LeBaron Jenney of Old Water Tower fame, fronting both Washington and Dearborn Streets. However, that parcel had other issues, so many of the State Street sites had many land-leases and subleases. The move of Carson Pirie Scott and Company into the Reliance Building, with its expansive windows and modern appearance for its era, may have established the company for its later move to State and Madison Streets.

In 1904, the Schlesinger & Mayer store, located a block south of the Reliance Building and designed by architect Louis Sullivan, was completed. This outstanding building, now world renowned, which stretched the limits of materials and their plasticity to new proportions, allowed for maximum light and air, which were critical to a retailer wanting to display clothing and wares in the days when electricity was in its infancy. The large single-paned display windows fronting State and Madison Streets are framed in elaborate cast-iron ornament, which appears effortless as it wraps around the display windows, often described like picture frames, extending to the top of the second floor, with its beautiful scrolling naturalistic ornament derived from the seed pod and forms in nature. Its corner entry and rotunda are treated in the same format but curving and encompassing a delicate skin, where the cast-iron ornament repeats and the pattern's strength diminishes to a delicate overlay, exposing the curving plate-glass window surface below and beyond. It invites the most curious and the most seasoned into this "work of art and architecture." The Madison Street façade, with its subtle large bay and canopy, undulates outward to further engage the shopper. This window bay was to be a feature along the State Street façade as well, but the City of Chicago had been threatening removal of these components of the building if a fee for the public right-of-way was not charged. This resulted in an agreement, but the challenges of the undulating base led to a more streamlined approach of a flattened wall, extending outward from the upper floors clad in terra cotta on the State Street façade of the store.

Above the ornamental cast iron, originally to be in bronze, was designed a creamy white terra-cotta façade with delicate vertical bands of ornament. This terra cotta was originally to be executed in white marble but changed to white terra cotta due to expense. These horizontal bands framed the upper-floor broad Chicago-style windows, with a fixed central panel and two smaller lights of glass. This design approach gave the building a strong horizontal focus, making the entire composition a powerful solution to a modern department store and quite in contrast to the newly constructed Marshall Field store to the north, with its more classical approach to the same program and use. An elaborate top floor of the Schlesinger & Mayer building with its fascia and cornice topped the department store with a colonnade of glass and terra cotta and an elaborate projecting cornice. This cantilevering cornice gave the building's top a defined end, further clarifying a base, shaft and cornice or top of the building—a tripartite system to architecture best executed by Louis Sullivan. The building is a masterpiece of the Chicago Commercial style or Chicago School of Architecture, where a building's metal or steel structure is clearly expressed and articulated on the façade. The interior of the store is clean-lined and has slender columns. Decorative capitals in Sullivan's naturalistic style pierce the sales floors in regular intervals but without the heaviness of the more lavish examples expressed in other department stores along State Street.

In 1904, at the completion of the building, Schlesinger & Mayer sold the building and its contents to Henry Selfridge, and for a period of four months, the enterprise became the H.G. Selfridge & Company store. Selfridge, a former partner in the Marshall Field store, became unhappy with his move, but through his associates and former partners of Field, mainly John G. Shedd (of the Shedd Aquarium fame in Chicago), he was able to negotiate a deal with Samuel Pirie resulting in Carson Pirie Scott being able to take possession of the building at a time when the firm may have been squeezed out of the retailing business on State Street. This was all executed in three rooms within the old Illinois State Bank Building on LaSalle Street, with Shedd in the central room and Selfridge and Pirie in separate isolated rooms. It was said that Selfridge made a tidy profit, outfoxing the Scotsmen, while also selling the land under the store to a nearby landowner and eventually transferring to Marshall Field I and later to the Field Museum of Natural History, which owned the land under the Carson's building until the early 1980s.

Carson Pirie Scott and Company was always a trendsetter, and its new building by Louis Sullivan may have furthered that image. The store always had a great personality: hip, modern and to the point. Its reputation in the 1960s was clean, affordable within reason, stylish and with the times. It was essentially how people may view a nameplate like Bloomingdale's today. The building and the department store became synonymous with each other, a landmark store in a landmark building, something to be celebrated and unique and differing from its many other branch stores.

Its friendly rivalry with Marshall Field was best seen when both would stage cultural in-store promotional events and trade fairs. Field's would stage the "British Showcase," where most everything had a British bent, including many of the items for sale. A variation of the "Changing of the Guard at Buckingham Palace" was staged at multiple times of the day in the State Street rooms, while high tea was served in the Walnut Room on the seventh floor. One occasion even brought a visit from Prince Charles, Prince of Wales, to Marshall Field. Meanwhile, Carson's had an event called "Mediterrenea" in its store, featuring wares from Italy, Greece, Turkey and the Mediterranean region. While the "Changing of the Guard" occurred at Field's, scantily clad belly dancers from Greece skirted and danced up and down the marble main-floor aisles of Carson's. They truly constituted a different approach to retailing and a store.

My own personal memories of Carson Pirie Scott are tied to my family and certain preferences for shopping. My mother, Martha Ward Miller, loved shopping on State Street, and we both visited the many stores on a regular basis. This was an unusual practice, as most individuals liked one store over another. My mother preferred Marshall Field overall to Carson's, opting to have dinner each Thursday evening with me in the Walnut Room or Bowlings Restaurant after teaching at the Chicago Board of Education headquarters on LaSalle and Wacker. My father and stepmother preferred Carson's for everything, including modern Scandinavian furniture, along with Baskin's and the former sporting goods shop Abercrombie & Fitch for clothes, which supplied outdoorsmen with clothing and gear—much different than the company with the current name. Maurice Rothschild's was a place for shirts for me when I was younger, as the service was outstanding and my mother loved that store. My dad would always take me to Wieboldt's for children's shoes. Goldblatt's, a giant discount retailer, would have the regular "designer sales" of everything from the New York stores at half the price yearly, which became another place to visit for most working mothers.

Christmas was a great time when all the stores outdid themselves with "Christmas Windows" of various themes all the way down State Street, along with objects wrapped or illuminated in lights. Field's took the cake on decorations with the thirteen-story atrium and the six-story Tiffany dome atrium ablaze in decorations. The exterior of the store would have large blinking snowflakes, decorative trumpets or horns and Christmas trees atop the entry canopies, in addition to the decorations throughout the store and, of course, the Great Tree in the Walnut Room.

Carson's had outlandish decorations, including an assembly of a European town with illumination behind that would integrate with the window theme or format. It was three stories tall and placed atop the cast-iron ornament of the lower floors fronting State Street, concealing the lower floors of the building with this illuminated glass-like colored façade of a townscape. A large figure or object, from a nativity window to a nutcracker, extending many stories in height, would often appear atop the corner entry at State and Madison. Carson's interior would be filled with purely decorative crystal chandeliers for the season, garlands and trees packed to the ceiling for the holidays. Carson's also had an eighth-floor auditorium for a Santa's Village display, complete with penguins, igloos and a good blast of air conditioning to greet you at the door, giving the effect of the North Pole, complete with photos with Santa. The line was a quarter of the length of the one to see Santa at Marshall Field.

Events were sometimes linked with celebrity visits connected with entertainment venues associated with the nearby Palmer House Hotel and the famous Empire Room, which featured top-name acts in nightly shows. It wasn't unusual to see big celebrities at Carson's, and the eighth-floor corridors between the Heather House Restaurant and lounges were lined with celebrity appearance photos of their time at Carson's.

Carson Pirie Scott also had a tremendous presence in the food, furniture and carpeting businesses. The Tartan Tray was a popular presence in the

State Street store, as well as at O'Hare Airport, where Carson's supplied the terminals and some of the airlines with food concessions. In addition, Honey Bear Farm in Lake Delavan, Wisconsin, supplied the stores with its own label of cured meats, cheeses and, of course, honey and baked products. Customers were encouraged to visit the working farm, which I remember doing one summer in the 1970s.

Carson Pirie Scott on State Street had the ability to transform itself into many different things over time. It was a Chicago institution based in a building of worldwide recognition, and it used every opportunity to promote the building, often injecting architecture into other promotional events. The State Street store and the building were inseparable, even appearing on catalogues, shopping bags and advertisements with the famed corner entry as its logo, much as the two clocks at Marshall Field often served as that store's logo. I personally remember the great excitement of my father and stepmother and the larger city when the building was bestowed with Chicago Landmark Designation in the early 1970s, following the tragic demise of Adler & Sullivan's Chicago Stock Exchange Building in 1971–72. The general euphoria was that Carson's would endure forever and would do it within a protected Chicago landmark. Contrary to public opinion, the company didn't feel it needed the landmark protection, and it did struggle to oppose the designation initially. The company later hired John Vinci in 1978–79, and a later owner hired Harboe and Associates to restore the façade of the building and the entry lobbies. This was a forward-thinking approach to a retail store in the late 1970s, when remodeling and modernization plans often prevailed in the quick-paced world of fashion.

Carson's on State Street is no longer, having closed in 2007. However, the company did maintain a significant building for almost one hundred years and kept it from demolition in a time when any older structure was fair game. It remained operating as its intended purpose, with all eight floors of commercial areas and the basement, later known as Corporate Level. It was part of an amazing collection of stores and institutions along State Street that created a real sense of arrival and destination. In a way, perhaps all these stores really did represent the city, its culture, its people, its architecture and its values.

Ward Miller
President and Executive Director of Preservation Chicago
Former Executive Director of the Richard Nickel Committee

Acknowledgements

Gratitude is one of the least articulate of the emotions, especially when it is deep.
—Felix Frankfurter, former associate justice of the Supreme Court of the
United States

Ialways dislike writing acknowledgements for my books. This is most certainly not due to any lack of appreciation, but it's because there are so very many people who contribute to the process, in ways both large and small, that I feel inadequate and tongue-tied when the time comes to thank them all. Writing is never a solitary undertaking, despite what the stereotypes would lead you to believe.

With this in mind, I'd like to thank everyone who contributed time, information, anecdotes, photos, memorabilia or moral support during this project. If I've missed anyone, please know I haven't forgotten your contribution, even if I have neglected to include your name here. To begin, I'd like to thank all the great folks at The History Press, for there would be no book without them. Ben Gibson has the patience of a saint and an eye for a great story, and Hilary Parrish does an amazing job of polishing my words and making me sound darn near coherent. The publicity team—especially Katie Parry—is always there to help at a moment's notice. Thanks to all of you!

For research assistance, I turned to the helpful staff at the Chicago History Museum, the Lee County Historical Society and the Art Institute of Chicago. They were each gracious and accommodating and helped me to make sense of the sometimes muddled history of the great store's founders.

Most importantly, I owe a huge debt of gratitude to Ward Miller and Jim McKay, who gave so unselfishly of their time, resources and ideas as this book evolved. Guys, I can't tell you how much your friendship and support means to me. I can only hope the finished product is worthy of the time and effort you invested in the project.

And last, but certainly not least, I'd like to thank Pete Rimsa—my husband, photographer, Photoshop wizard, dinner procurer and best friend for suffering through yet another book with me.

Chapter 1

FROM NORTHERN IRELAND TO NORTHERN ILLINOIS

The true adventurer goes forth aimless and uncalculating to meet and greet unknown fate.
—*O. Henry*

The mid-nineteenth century was a painful and desperate time throughout many parts of Europe. A widespread blight wiped out vast numbers of potato crops that served as the primary dietary staple for millions of peasants and laborers, causing mass starvation. The crisis all began with a simple fungus-like organism known as *Phytophthora infestans.* The disease probably had its origins high in the Andean rainforests of South America before it made its debut in 1843 on the eastern seaboard of the United States, most notably around New York and Philadelphia. From there, the killer likely hitched a ride across the Atlantic in 1845 aboard a schooner bound for Belgium with a shipment of seed potatoes. Once ashore, it quickly worked its cruel magic across the continent, its spores spreading unfettered on the prevailing winds. The afflicted crops would burst from the ground, apparently healthy and abundant, before suddenly collapsing in a blackened moldy heap.

Nowhere was the crisis more apparent than in Ireland and the Scottish Highlands. Even though large areas of Europe and the United States were impacted, the blight era is often referred to as the "Irish potato famine." Due to the politics of the time, most Irish families lived on small farms owned by British Protestants. In fact, up until the early 1900s, approximately 97 percent of the land in Ireland was held by absentee landowners. Most of the property had been bequeathed to supporters of the British monarchy in an attempt to eradicate Catholicism from Ireland, and the poverty-stricken residents eked out a subsistence living by growing crops of wheat, barley and oats for their wealthy masters. These crops were sold for a handsome profit, while the farmers and their families typically survived on a tiny garden plot of humble spuds.

When the blight struck in all its fury and the potatoes rotted in the ground, the Irish had nowhere to turn for relief. Their families were starving, but if they did not hand over all the grain crops to pay their rents, the landowners would quickly evict them and turn the land into more valuable grazing pastures as the British demand for meat increased. Sadly, some landlords evicted tenant farmers practically at whim. Hundreds of thousands of these now-homeless poor were loaded into transatlantic schooners with the promise of a better life in America. Unfortunately, the already sick and starving wretches fared no better at sea on the meager rations, and so many died during the voyages that these vessels became known as "coffin ships." It has been estimated that more than one million people died from starvation or starvation-related disease during the seven-year period (1845–52) roughly encompassing the famine, and more than one million emigrated. Other researchers, however, claim that those statistics are egregiously low, and the toll was actually a great deal higher. In fact, a growing number of historians have charged that the blight, while accidental, quickly turned into a tool of genocide for a British aristocracy eager to purge the land of Catholics. The Earl of Lucan, who owned more than sixty thousand acres, purportedly said he "would not breed paupers to pay priests" when asked to explain why he was evicting his dying and malnourished tenants. It was against this backdrop of social upheaval and tragedy that two young Scotsmen emerged with a dream for a better life.

John Thomas Pirie was born on August 26, 1827, in Errol, Scotland, a picturesque village on the banks of the Tay River. His father, Allan A. Pirie, was an industrious cabinetmaker who instilled a strong work ethic in his son. When John Thomas reached his early teens, he moved to Newry, Ireland, to apprentice in the dry goods business under the watchful eye of his maternal uncle, Henry Hawkins. Uncle Henry was a fine teacher, and soon young John was hired away to serve as a department head at John Arnott & Company, a prestigious dry goods establishment in the bustling city of Belfast. John was a natural at the trade, and his skills as both a shrewd buyer and a practiced salesman earned him competitive offers from the finest firms. But although his career was advancing nicely, John yearned to strike out on his own.

One day, he blurted out his thoughts to his best mate, a young man named Samuel Carson, whom he had befriended back in the days at Uncle Henry's firm in Newry. Carson was enthusiastic, and soon the two pooled their meager savings and opened a small dry goods firm of their own in Cookstown, Ireland, a fast-growing hamlet about fifty miles west of Belfast. Cookstown was a place of great commerce and industry. Two railroads—the Great Northern and the London Midland and Scottish Railway—each established terminals in the town to transport goods and produce to Cookstown's famous market. It was also an important center for the linen-making industry. Various mills and factories spun, bleached and wove the golden flax into delicate garments and household linens that were coveted around the globe. It held this distinction until the mid-1960s, when an influx of cheaper Asian imports flooded the market and reduced demand. Even today, however, Irish linen is still considered the finest in the world.

Cookstown seemed like the perfect place for a dry goods store, as it was somewhat removed from the deadly drama playing out across the rest of the land. The new partners did reasonably well, but they still yearned for more opportunity than the oppressive and depressed country had to offer at the time. They read with great interest the letters they received from Robert Murray, a close mutual friend who had moved across the ocean to the United States. Murray had opened a small dry goods store in Peru, Illinois, and spoke glowingly about the limitless opportunities available in the young American frontier. Carson and Pirie were rootless and restless and decided to join the swelling ranks of those heading abroad to seek a brighter future. It was with this mixture of recklessness and youthful optimism that they closed up the Cookstown shop—forfeiting most of the year's rent they had paid in advance—said goodbye to family and friends and boarded a steamer bound for Philadelphia to start a new life.

The ship they chose for their journey was named after its city of destination, and it was embarking on its maiden voyage. The SS *City of Philadelphia* was a twenty-two-ton iron-hulled single-screw passenger ship built for the Liverpool and Philadelphia Steamship Company, commonly known as the Inman Line. The *Philadelphia* was just the third ship in the young company's fleet and was intended to help cement the Inman Line's reputation as a modern and efficient passenger carrier. Most of its competitors still ran wooden paddle steamers or sailing packets, and so the iron-hulled and screw-propelled liner appeared quite modern indeed. It steamed out of Liverpool on Wednesday, August 29, 1854, with a load of more than six hundred emigrants looking toward an uncertain but hopeful future. Spirits were high;

according to passenger J.W. Gadsby, "For six days we were favored with fine weather, clear skies, and smooth seas…we enjoyed all the pleasure, and none of the usual discomforts, of an Atlantic voyage."

Although the passengers were happy and carefree, Captain Robert Leitch of the *Philadelphia* had fewer reasons for celebration. The six compasses aboard ship were acting oddly and often varied from one another by a range of several degrees. They had been carefully calibrated in London and Glasgow, but it appeared that no one had gone to proper lengths to ensure their accuracy on board a vessel constructed almost entirely of iron. By the seventh day, the ship was approximately thirty to forty miles off course and trapped in blinding rain and dense fog. In spite of this, it appears that the captain made no attempt to slow his speed and forged ahead at about twelve knots, nearly the limit for the weighty behemoth. Just before midnight on September 6, the sleeping passengers were jolted awake by a massive concussion; the *Philadelphia* had struck a rocky shoal off the coast of Cape Race in southeastern Newfoundland. It's worth noting that most anecdotal accounts, including a recorded eyewitness description by passenger Gadsby, mention the date of sinking as September 24, but a lawsuit filed later that year for damaged freight set the date as September 6; this date coincides with Gadsby's chronological recount of the voyage and the distance and speed traveled. The September 24 date was most likely a misprint that simply was handed down and repeated as fact over time.

In any case, the ship and its passengers were in grave danger as icy water poured unabated into a large gash in the port hull. Captain Leitch knew that they were still quite far from land, and the shoal was surrounded by deep water on each side. With little time to spare, he made a quick and fortuitous decision: the crew reversed the engine, backed the wounded liner off the rocks and then sped full ahead for the shallows of Chance Cove, about seven and a half miles to the north. The mortally wounded ship plowed into the cove just as the second hold compartment filled with water and dragged the vessel down onto the rocky bottom. It settled upright, its upper decks securely above water. The terrified, hysterical passengers began to calm as they realized they were, against all odds, safe and sound. With most of the danger averted, the crew was able to load and lower the lifeboats slowly and methodically and ferry passengers to the nearby shore. There were not sufficient lifeboats to hold all the passengers—maritime regulations wouldn't require that until the *Titanic* tragedy nearly sixty years later—but the crew made multiple trips back and forth, and by dawn, the ship was completely evacuated without any loss of life. The *Philadelphia*, however, was a total loss.

The area was desolate, and the survivors had to camp on the beach for a few days until the first rescue ship, the mail steamer *Victoria*, arrived on the scene. Its captain bartered an agreement with Captain Leitch to transport people to the nearby port of St. John's, Newfoundland, for the price of five dollars a head. Only about half the passengers would fit onto the small ship, so the *Victoria* returned the following day for the remainder of the castaways. From St. John's, the stranded travelers dispersed to various locales via a number of different ships; it's not clear how Carson and Pirie continued their voyage, but they apparently found their way to New York and not their original destination of Philadelphia. And, in all the confusion, they had lost the address of their friend Robert Murray. New York City suited the young men just fine, however, and both quickly found work at James Beck & Co., one of the many wholesale dry goods firms that flourished in the metropolis. But they knew it was just a stopping point in their journey; their dream of opening their own firm remained strong in their minds and hearts.

After a few months of saving money and acclimating to their adopted country, they were finally able to reestablish contact with Murray, and the budding entrepreneurs moved west to the Illinois River town of LaSalle, Illinois. At that time, the area was heavily populated with Irish immigrants who had come seeking construction jobs on the new Illinois and Michigan Canal. The canal, which was completed in 1848, was an engineering marvel that clawed through ninety-six miles of prairie land to connect the Chicago and Illinois Rivers, thus opening a continuous shipping channel that ran from the East Coast, through the Great Lakes and down the Mississippi to the Gulf of Mexico. As a result, the sleepy fur-trading settlement of Chicago blossomed into a world-class city and transportation hub, and the numerous small towns that dotted the landscape along the rivers and canal grew as well. Carson and Pirie immediately opened a tiny rented shop in LaSalle, using merchandise they acquired from Murray, whose dry goods store was prospering in the nearby river town of Peru. But it, too, was just a temporary stop on their path to bigger things.

By early 1855, less than a year after they had sailed from Liverpool, the partners were ready to open a real store, one that would showcase their talents and aspirations. They just needed to find the right location. As Samuel Carson once recounted:

> *We found a new pattern of life forming in the midlands of America, Illinois, and set out to find the best location, visiting the numerous towns in the search. Finally I came to Amboy, the Northern Division headquarters*

Amboy, Illinois, was a bustling railroad town and the Northern Division headquarters for the Illinois Central Railroad when Samuel Carson decided it was a perfect location for a dry goods store in 1855. *Photo by Peter Rimsa.*

Samuel Carson rented the only available building in Amboy, a recently closed saloon. The building now houses the Long Branch Saloon. *Photo by Peter Rimsa.*

of the Illinois Central Railroad, about thirty miles north of LaSalle. It had been incorporated the year before [1854] with a population of 1,994 and seemed certain for prosperous growth. When I returned to LaSalle, John T. Pirie was in the midst of a sale. I do not remember whether he completed it. "John, I've found it. I've found it!" I told him. We quickly agreed on the move. At first I was unable to find a building, but as I was about to leave, a citizen told me the vigilance committee was about to close a saloon. It would be available tomorrow, he said.

And so, in the summer of 1855, "Carson & Pirie's One Price Cheap Cash Store" opened for a bustling first day of business in a rundown saloon with a rowdy past. It would do, however, until better accommodations came along. The first day's take was $40—quite a handsome sum, considering the average salary for a typical working man was just over $300 per year at the time. The young men had been in America for only eight short months, and they were already on the road to realizing their dream. "We set out to learn what the people wanted and soon had the better trade of the town. In a few months we outgrew the former saloon and bought a nearby building for $2,500, of which $1,900 was in notes. It caused considerable comment when the notes were paid before falling due," observed Carson. "At the end of the year we showed a profit of $2,500."

On the heels of such an auspicious start, the young partners eagerly planned to expand their business model to other prairie towns. But with the beginnings of such an empire, they would need help they could trust. In early 1856, Samuel traveled back to Ireland. While visiting the old country, Carson accomplished two very important feats: first, he convinced some old family friends, brothers George and Robert Scott, to come to Illinois and run the Amboy store, thus freeing Carson and Pirie to travel about and seek out new opportunities. And, most importantly, he married his longtime sweetheart—who also happened to be his partner's sister. Samuel Carson and Elizabeth "Betsey" Pirie were wedded on February 22, 1856, at a small church in Newry, Ireland. Sam and Betsey returned to Amboy that spring, but the family tree wasn't yet done branching.

In 1857, John Pirie also married—and, in what must have been a déjà vu moment for the families, he married *his* partner's sister, Sarah Carson. Sarah had traveled to the United States with Samuel and Betsey in 1856 and soon stole John's heart. The Piries went on to have seven children and named them in a manner guaranteed to confuse genealogists and historians for centuries to come. Their oldest son, born in 1864, was named Samuel Carson Pirie, or S.C., in honor of Pirie's partner. Their third daughter, Sarah, was born in 1866 and named after her mother. In 1871, John T. Jr. was born. The other children were firstborn Mary (1860), Margaret (1862), Allan (1878, named after his paternal grandfather) and finally Gordon (1880).

Sam and Betsey were decidedly less prolific. In fact, they were childless. Some sources claim they had one child—a daughter named Anna—who was reportedly disowned when she married a man named Chandler whom her family greatly disliked. Anna, however, was Sam's niece, the daughter of his older brother Andrew. Anna was a young headstrong teen when Andrew, his wife, Fanny, and their five children settled in Amboy during the 1860s along with the rest of the clan. It's not known if she was indeed disowned, but she did apparently marry into the Chandler family and spent the rest of her life in the Amboy area. To add to the muddled family history, Andrew and Fanny also had a son whom they named Samuel, and he followed his uncle into the dry goods business. Many historical accounts erroneously identify him as Sam's son rather than his nephew. And, of course, when that Samuel grew up and got married, he named *his* firstborn son Samuel. In case you've lost count, that adds up to three Samuel Carsons and one Samuel Carson Pirie, each of whom was associated with the family business at one point or another.

Life in Amboy was, by all accounts, a happy time for the partners. Although they had been staunch Presbyterians in Ireland, they soon became active congregants in Amboy's newly formed First Baptist Church. The church had gotten its start just a few months before Carson and Pirie moved to town, and its first services were held in a little schoolhouse on West Main Street. By 1857, however, the congregation had grown sufficiently to support the construction of a beautiful new building on Mason Avenue. The stately wooden structure featured a tall belfry and steeple containing a massive bell that weighed more than eight hundred pounds. The church stood proudly in the heart of town until it was destroyed by fire one bitter cold morning in February 1923. All that remained was a rescued Bible, some silverware and the enormous bell that was lying silent in the ruins. The parishioners were undeterred, however, and quickly began construction on a new, larger brick building, which was officially dedicated in July 1924 and remains active to this day. The historic bell, retrieved from the ashes and reinstalled in the new building, still calls the faithful to Sunday services.

Despite their dedication to work and church, the partners did find some time to relax. Together, they purchased a farm about two miles east of Amboy where they and their extended families could enjoy the charming

A plaque on the wall of the Long Branch Saloon commemorates the location as the first store of Carson and Pirie. *Photo by Peter Rimsa.*

pastoral countryside. An old-time resident of the area, Mr. W.H. Badger, once recalled his amusement at watching the distinguished businessmen act the part of rural farmers: "The road to the farm passed by the schoolhouse where I went to school. We boys laughed with delight whenever Mr. Carson or Mr. Pirie rode the old grey mare out to the farm, for they rode with short stirrups, rising up and down as the mare trotted along. They were great merchants, but would hardly shine in a Wild West Rodeo."

Indeed, although they worked diligently to provide all the necessities a prairie family might need, Carson and Pirie were savvy enough to know that even a poor farmer's wife might covet a bit of finery when finances allowed. With that in mind, the Amboy store soon expanded beyond the rough calicos and utilitarian garments typical of local merchants. Sarah and Betsey urged their husbands to add a millinery department on the unused second floor, and it was a grand success. Soon, the store gained a reputation as a fashion emporium, and business boomed. It was time to expand!

The partners opened new locations in Mendota and Galena in 1857, followed by Polo in 1858 and finally Sterling in 1859, arguably making Carson and Pirie the nation's first chain department store. But although the expansion was successful, it wasn't without anxiety. The Great Panic of 1857—the world's first global economic crisis— rocked the country's financial stability as banks and railroads foundered. Land prices dropped precipitously, and many farmers found themselves owing more in taxes than their vast homesteads were worth. To make matters worse, the price of grain plummeted as well, tumbling from a high of $2.19 a bushel in 1855 to a mere $0.80 in 1857. People could not cover their debts, and foreclosures were rampant. Carson and Pirie reluctantly issued a strict cash-only policy, and sales in the Amboy store declined from a robust average of $100 per day down to as little as $12. Eventually, however, the economy struggled back, and the fledgling firm survived in large part due to the shrewd business judgment of the principals. By 1859, the stores were once again profitable, and George and Robert Scott were rewarded with a small partnership stake.

Although each of the men worked tirelessly and displayed a strong Protestant ethic, they also demanded the same of their hired associates. The company's first official employee policy enumerated both the duties and personal characteristics that the partners expected from their staff:

> *Store must be open from 6 a.m. to 9 p.m. the year round. Store must be swept; counters, base shelves, and showcases dusted; lamps trimmed, filled and chimneys cleaned; pens made; doors and windows opened; a pail of*

In 1929, Amboy welcomed Carson Pirie Scott and Company executives to town for the company's Diamond Jubilee. This photo is a costumed reenactment of shoppers at the original store.

water, also a bucket of coal brought in before breakfast if there is time to do so and attend to customers who call. Store must not be opened on the Sabbath day unless necessary, and then only for a few minutes. The employee who is in the habit of smoking Spanish cigars, being shaved at the barber's, going to dances and other places of amusement will surely give his employer reasons to be suspicious of his integrity and honesty. Each employee must not pay less than $5 per year to the church and must attend Sunday School regularly. Men employees are given one evening a week for courting and two if they go to the prayer meeting. After fourteen hours of work in the store, leisure time should be spent mostly in reading.

At the beginning of 1860, the ominous rumblings of the impending Civil War had begun. The chasm between slaveholding Southern states and the abolitionist North was growing rapidly, and in December of that year, South Carolina became the first to secede from the Union. The ensuing war years exacted a brutal price on the nation in terms of lost lives and economic devastation, especially in Confederate states. In parts of the more heavily industrialized North, however, the bloody war actually acted as an economic stimulus. Perhaps nowhere was this more apparent than in Chicago. Already recognized as a shipping port and railroad hub, the young city was also one of the world's leading centers for iron and steel production. Iron ore mined in Michigan and Minnesota could be transported with relative ease by ore boats from the Lake Superior region down through Lake Michigan to the massive mills sprouting up along Chicago's southern boundaries. The nearly insatiable wartime demand for these materials attracted investors and laborers alike, and the population and manufacturing increases spurred the need for more railroads, which of course required yet more iron and steel to build.

But Chicago wasn't just a city of industry. The endless prairies to the north, west and south of the city contained some of the richest black soil in North America. Farms in the region burst forth with an abundance that amazed and thrilled the immigrant settlers, and by 1860, Illinois was the number-one producer in the country of both corn and wheat. The lush prairies also excelled as grazing land for livestock. Grain elevators and slaughterhouses dotted the landscape, and the bountiful harvests queued up in Chicago's rail yards and shipping docks awaiting distribution and transport to distant cities.

None of this was lost on Carson and Pirie. Although their frontier stores were performing admirably, they realized that the wholesale trade opportunities in the burgeoning city offered a promise of wealth and excitement well beyond the scope of anything they could hope to achieve in Amboy. And so, in early 1864, the men opened a wholesale operation at 20 Lake Street, in what was then the heart of Chicago's commercial district. It's not clear if they intended to leave the retail trade and Amboy behind, but fate forced their hand; on November 10, 1864, the store was destroyed in a raging fire that left five businesses gutted, with a total loss of $45,000—quite a large sum in those days. Although the outlying stores remained open for a few more years under the Scotts' management, by 1868 they were shuttered in favor of the Chicago business, and the Scott brothers joined Samuel and John in the city. It was just the beginning of a new empire that would be beyond anything the partners could have imagined.

Chapter 2

THE EARLY YEARS IN CHICAGO

*It is hopeless for the occasional visitor to try to keep up with Chicago—she
outgrows her prophecies faster than she can make them. She is always a novelty;
for she is never the Chicago you saw when you passed through the last time.*
—*Mark Twain*

Chicago in the late 1850s was a city with a dilemma. Thirty years
earlier, when the young state of Illinois first began to survey and plat
the area, the entire population amounted to fewer than 100 fur trappers
and traders who lived in crude shacks clustered near the muddy banks
of the Chicago River. By 1860, that number had exploded to more than
112,000 as eager settlers and fortune-hunters poured into the area from
points across the globe. Unfortunately, no one had yet addressed some of
the basic challenges posed by such unfettered growth. The city had sprung
from a prairie bog, and during the rainy season, frequent flooding created
a quagmire of standing water and mud deep enough to trap horses and
wagons. In response, the residents created wooden sidewalks and roads,
but their effectiveness was questionable. In June 1856, *Putnam's Monthly
Magazine* published a description: "Both carriage-way and sidewalks are
planked—stone being as yet too expensive a material, and too slowly laid
for this new and fast metropolis. In the spring of the year, the ground
asserts its original character of a swamp. The planks actually float, and,
as the heavy wagons pass along, ornamental jets of muddy water play on
the every side."

Sanitation was also a critical concern. The once-pristine but slow-moving Chicago River had become a foul open sewer filled with human waste, animal carcasses and slaughterhouse offal. Putrid, gag-inducing stenches blanketed the area like a shroud, especially during the broiling heat of summer. These odors were known as "miasmas" and were believed to be poisonous vapors filled with particles of decomposed matter that caused many common diseases. It certainly wouldn't have been hard to imagine. Cholera was rampant; originally a disease limited to South Asia, it reached the United States in the 1830s and spread to Chicago soon thereafter. In an attempt to fight the spread of infection, authorities created the Chicago Board of Health in 1835, and small temporary hospitals designed to isolate cholera, typhoid and smallpox victims dotted the area. In spite of these efforts, however, outbreaks were frequent and deadly. In the early 1850s, a cholera pandemic killed an estimated 5.5 percent of the city's population. The *Chicago Tribune* lamented the lack of sanitation in an 1854 editorial:

> *So many of the streets, the alleys, and the gutters, are ankle deep in festering corruption and rottenness; there are so many choked up drains and unmanageable sewers; there are such immense piles of garbage and filth at the back of Hotels Restaurants and Oyster Saloons; and there is yet so much suffering and destitution among the poorer portion of our citizens and the emigrants daily arriving here; there is, in one word, so much of what ought not to be, and so little of what ought to be, in the sanitary condition of our city.*

Perhaps nowhere were these problems more obvious than along Lake Street, the city's "street of merchants." The fast-growing commercial district squatted a short distance from the south bank of the river's main stem, near the remains of the long-abandoned Fort Dearborn. Shoppers arriving via carriage would struggle to navigate the muddy, rutted thoroughfare, usually with handkerchiefs pressed tightly against their faces as they hurried about their business. Pranksters left crudely lettered signs at some of the worst mud holes, such as "this way to China!" and "No bottom." Beautiful multistory marble-fronted buildings sprouted incongruently from the muck alongside shabby wooden structures erected decades earlier, but the filth and stench discouraged all but the most necessary outings. Public officials knew that drastic measures were needed. And so, in a remarkable feat of engineering, the city began the arduous task of rising from the mire.

Earlier attempts at surface grading to enhance drainage had failed; the flat landscape simply sat too near the level of Lake Michigan for gravity to have the necessary effect. In 1855, the newly created Chicago Board of Sewerage Commissioners finally came up with a plan; if they couldn't lower the lake, they would raise the town! They hired a Boston engineer named Ellis Sylvester Chesbrough to study the situation. Under Chesbrough's guidance, the city would create the first comprehensive storm and sewage system in the country. And thus began the monumental task of lifting or moving existing buildings to create a new street grade an average of ten feet higher than the original settlement. Most of the older wooden structures, especially houses, were simply picked up, placed on rollers and dragged to the outskirts. A visitor named David Macrae recorded his experiences in the suddenly mobile city: "Never a day passed that I did not meet one or more houses shifting their quarters. One day I met nine." The new multistory brick and marble commercial structures, however, posed a bit more of a challenge. A consortium of engineers—including James Brown of Boston, Chicagoan James Hollingsworth and a newcomer from New York named George Pullman—devised an ingenious if labor-intensive method of accomplishing the task. Workers dug trenches under the buildings and placed hundreds, sometimes thousands, of jackscrews under the existing foundations. And then, with painstaking precision, they would slowly lift the buildings to their desired elevations.

Once the building was raised up, laborers laid sewer pipes underneath, covered them with earth dredged from the river and constructed new foundation walls. Amazingly, the whole process was usually performed without closing the business or removing any of the contents. In fact, most visitors barely noticed the engineering exploits being performed under their feet. One inattentive guest at the Tremont House hotel was reportedly confounded by the fact that during his stay, the front staircase that led from the street to the hotel lobby grew steeper by the day. Perhaps the most remarkable feat occurred in 1860, when engineers simultaneously raised half a city block on Lake Street consisting of four- and five-story brick and stone buildings with a combined estimated weight of thirty-five thousand tons. In that event, thousands of spectators turned out to watch, and they were briefly allowed to walk under the buildings among the jacks.

This was the Chicago that Carson and Pirie embraced in 1864. Their new wholesale operation at 20 Lake Street was located on a block that had been recently graded and had its wooden structures removed. The commercial district, while cramped and still positioned near the odorous riverfront, had been much improved over the past decade, and business was brisk. Dozens of other dry goods wholesalers,

CATALOGUE
OF
DIAMONDS
WATCHES
JEWELRY
SILVERWARE
1906

CARSON, PIRIE
SCOTT & COMPANY
CHICAGO

Carson's had a vibrant wholesale division in Chicago for more than one hundred years.

including the firm of Farwell, Field & Company—the precursor to Marshall Field & Company—lined the street. Most had at least a small retail shop at the front of their businesses, and Carson and Pirie yearned to do the same, but they were already spread very thin in trying to get the wholesale business up and running. Retail would have to wait.

But in spite of their heavy workload, the partners managed to remain active participants in the Baptist Church. Although the extended Carson and Pirie clans stayed in the Amboy area, both men moved their immediate families to Chicago. It was there that they joined the North Baptist Church, then located at Dearborn and Ontario Streets. It was also at this church that Sam Carson first developed a close friendship with a young man named Andrew MacLeish.

MacLeish was a fellow Scotsman, born in 1838 in Glasgow to a family of dry goods merchants. Although his parents fervently hoped he would turn to the ministry, when young Andrew insisted on a career as a merchant, his father arranged for him to apprentice at Robert Webster & Sons, one of the best shops in Glasgow. But instead of returning to the family business after his training at Webster's, he decided to join his friend Edward Couper in London. Although his father was quite displeased with the plan, Andrew borrowed eight sovereigns—roughly $900 in today's money—from his older sister Agnes and headed off to seek his fortune.

Unfortunately, London didn't provide the riches that the boys had hoped for. After dreary weeks of searching for work, they found only modest positions with mediocre firms. Business was slow, and they were discouraged and broke. Surely, they thought, there must be a better place for two ambitious and talented young men such as themselves! About this time, Andrew and Edward received letters from Miss Lilias Young, a friend and coworker from their days at Webster's. She had moved with her family to the American frontier and wrote glowingly about her new home in the city of Chicago. It was a prosperous boomtown, she said, with abundant opportunities just ripe for the taking. After a brief discussion, the friends agreed to throw caution to the wind and strike out for America. After a quick trip back to Glasgow to bid farewell to their unhappy families, MacLeish and Couper boarded the iron steamship *City of New York* in the autumn of 1856 for their adventure into the unknown.

In those days, the trip from the dock at New York to the railroad terminal in Chicago was an arduous three-day journey. Railroad sleeper cars hadn't yet been introduced, so the passengers had to disembark each night to catch a few precious hours of sleep at towns along the way before continuing their journey in the morning. The terminal in Chicago, at the foot of Lake Street, was just an unroofed crude shed in 1856, planted forlornly in the still-muddy street. Nevertheless, the friends immediately embraced their new home and marveled at the city's potential for growth. MacLeish later wrote about his first night in Chicago: "I walked, with Miss Young, westward on Lake Street, out to the boundless prairie at Union Park." Although Andrew quickly found employment at J.B. Shay, one of the dry goods merchants on Lake Street, he suffered "a breakdown in health" in early 1858. The Young family had recently purchased a farm near Golconda, Illinois, the county seat of Pope County, and they invited MacLeish to join them. The tiny settlement at the southern tip of Illinois squats on the banks of the Ohio River and once served as a ferry point—known as Lusk's Ferry— across the river to Kentucky. Today, much of the area is part of the Shawnee National Forest, but at that time, the deeply forested rolling and rocky hills were dotted with small farms. Unfortunately, due to over-farming and erosion, many of these farms offered meager harvests at best. Although MacLeish and the Youngs struggled mightily to succeed, their career in agriculture was doomed to failure. The well-educated Andrew accepted a brief position as schoolmaster in the district as the Young family planned a return to the more prosperous life in Chicago. Lilias, however, did not return with her family; instead, on Christmas Day 1858, she became Mrs. Andrew MacLeish in a small ceremony at a neighboring farmhouse.

By the spring of 1859, the newlyweds had seen enough of the rural lifestyle. MacLeish's teaching contract was up, and he politely declined to renew it. Instead, they headed back to Chicago, where Andrew's old job with J.B. Shay still awaited him. The couple moved to a modest apartment on Erie Street and settled into the domestic life. By all accounts, it was a happy time; their first child, Lily, was born just as the country moved into the Civil War, and a second daughter, Blanche, followed three years later. It was also during this time that the family joined the North Baptist Church, where Andrew would eventually meet Sam Carson.

As the years passed, however, MacLeish was becoming increasingly disappointed in his employment. Despite being made a partner at Shay's, money was tight. After a few difficult years, he withdrew from the partnership and briefly accepted a position with Field, Leiter & Company, the successor of Farwell & Field. Still dissatisfied and restless, MacLeish considered moving his family back to the country, where the cost of living was cheaper. Perhaps he could start his own small dry goods store and create a better life for his wife and children. He confided his plans to his trusted friend from

RDAY, MAY 4, 1867.

Dry Goods.

NEW

DRY GOODS STORE.

Ladies Attention!

CARSON, PIRIE & CO.,

WILL OPEN THE STORE

No. 136 Lake-st.,

ON

WEDNESDAY MAY 8TH,

WITH A FRESH,

New and Desirable Stock

OF

**Staple and Fancy Dry Goods,
including Dress Trimmings,
Ribbons, Laces, &c., &c.**

GOODS ALL NEW !

NO HARD STOCK!

**Newest Fabrics,
Latest Styles,
Cheapest Prices.**

Do not purchase till you see our Stock. Bargains in every thing.

136 - 136 - 136

136 LAKE-ST.

Our Jobbing Business at 20 Lake st., as formerly.

A. McLEISH,

Desires to notify his friends and acquaintances that he has entered into copartnership with

CARSON, PIRIE & CO.,

IN THE

Retail Dry Goods Business,

AT

No. 136 Lake-st.,

He will be happy to see them there on our opening our new premises,

Next Wednesday, May 8th.

church, Samuel Carson. As it turned out, Carson had a better idea. He and Pirie had long wanted to enter the retail business in Chicago but simply didn't have the manpower. Pirie was now spending most of his time in New York managing the firm's new foreign buying offices in England, France and Germany. Carson and the Scott brothers had their hands full running the Chicago wholesale trade and maintaining the handful of stores still open in the prairie towns. Carson knew and trusted MacLeish and believed he was just the man to start up a retail establishment for the firm. And so, in early 1867, MacLeish accepted a partnership in Carson, Pirie and Company.

Their first Chicago retail store opened in May of that year at 136 Lake Street. It wouldn't remain at that location for long, though. At about that time, the former dry goods merchant turned real estate magnate Potter Palmer began buying up huge tracts of land on nearby State Street. Palmer believed that Lake Street's days as a commercial center were numbered. It was too close to the still-smelly river and hemmed in between railroad tracks and the riverbank. There was no room for growth and little opportunity for significant improvement. State Street, on the other hand, had plenty of potential. It was then just a narrow and rutted lane lined with a slum of shanties, flophouses and cheap saloons, but the new railroad and streetcar lines all converged there, making it a convenient place to reach from any part of the city. Although many of his contemporaries openly mocked his plan, Palmer ignored their derision and bought every lot he could until he held title to most of the frontage property on State Street between Lake Street and Quincy Avenue to the south, a distance of three-quarters of a mile. He immediately tore down or set back each building he owned and persuaded his remaining neighbors to do the same so that

QUADRUPLE SILVER PLATED WARE.
Prices each.

No. **W677** Spoon, height 3¾ inches... $2.00

No. **W677** Cream, height 3¾ in......$2.00

No. **W677** Tea Pot. $3.50
Height 8 inches; capacity 6 half pints.

No. **W677** Sugar, height 6 inches....$2.25

No. **W667** Syrup and Plate, height 5¼ in...$2.25

No. **W677** Butter, height 5¼ in.....$2.25

No. **W677** Tea Set (6 pieces), satin, bright cut engraved; burnished handles and spouts; Spoon and Cream gold lined.... **$14.25**

No. **W654** Tea Set (6 pieces), raised and chased; burnished or butler finish......$21.00

Tea Pot, height 7½ in.; capacity 5¼ half pints $4.50	Cream Pitcher, height 4½ in.; gold lined $3.00	Sugar Bowl, height 5¾ in......................$3.50
Spoon Holder, height 4½ in.; gold lined 3.00	Butter Dish, height 5 in.... .... 3.50	Syrup Pitcher and Plate, height 5½ in. 3.50

Above: It used to be possible to purchase quadruple silver-plated teapots and accessories for less than five dollars.

Opposite: An advertisement for the 1867 opening of Carson's first Chicago retail location.

the once-narrow street was more than one hundred feet wide. Instead of a cramped and grimy horse path, State Street now had the ability to become a magnificent boulevard.

Palmer soon began construction on a huge new retail building at the corner of State and Washington Streets. The limestone and marble edifice towered six stories above the street, and the façade featured dramatic white Corinthian columns. The building was quickly dubbed "Palmer's Palace," and all it needed was a suitable tenant. By this point, Palmer had spent well over $2 million funding his dream of a new business district, and he knew that it would all be for naught if he couldn't convince the merchants to relocate. Luckily, he was able to entice his old friends Marshall Field and Levi Leiter to move their fast-growing business to his palatial building. Field and Leiter had purchased Palmer's dry goods firm years earlier and had grown it into the undisputed leader in Chicago's mercantile trade. And so, on Monday, October 12, 1868, Field's new store opened with a grand flourish. The *Chicago Tribune* gushed, "The formal opening by Field, Leiter and Company of Potter Palmer's new marble palace on the corner of Washington and State was the grandest affair of its kind which ever transpired even in Chicago, the city of grand affairs…[even] New York cannot boast such a gorgeous palace for the display of dry goods."

It quickly became clear that Palmer's vision was right on the money. Shoppers and gawkers alike flocked to the new store to witness the awe-inspiring first-floor retail emporium. The stylishly rounded counters were constructed of satiny dark walnut, dramatically framed against a backdrop of white frescoed walls. New gas lighting fixtures cast a pleasant warm glow across the room—nothing like the dreary and dark establishments of the past. And the vast selection of merchandise was attractively displayed as helpful and polite associates stood ready to assist. Field himself was well liked and highly regarded as an ethical and visionary businessman. In fact, legend has it that "What would Field do?" became a common refrain among his merchant peers. It came as little surprise, therefore, when one store after another closed its doors on Lake Street and followed Field to the new business district on State.

Carson and Pirie were no exception. In late 1868, a raging fire caused heavy damage to their wholesale operation at 20 Lake Street, forcing them to relocate that business to a temporary home at Wabash and Randolph. In early 1869, they packed up the retail store at 136 Lake and moved to a new building on the west side of State Street, just north of Madison and just a short walk from Field's. And shortly thereafter, they consolidated the

NOTICE

 IN handing you this Catalogue, in which we have shown you most of the illustrations photographed direct from the goods, we believe we have placed these articles before you in a manner that will be not only novel, but at the same time will give you an idea of exactly how the articles look. We have spent a great deal of time and expense in getting up this book and we ask you to keep it before you so that it may be handy to show to your customers.

To facilitate the filling of orders, please use the order blank inserted in the Catalogue, for Jewelry exclusively, especially in December. In ordering Rings, to get exact size, use the ring gauge inserted in Catalogue, or one will be sent on application. If order is received late in December and the particular item is sold out, we will substitute a very similar one unless ordered not to do so.

Prices and discounts on all lines subject to change. Please do not cut illustrations from this book.

CARSON PIRIE SCOTT & CO.

Carson's provided detailed and illustrated catalogues to its customers to use as sales tools.

wholesale business into the upper floors on State, above their beautiful new retail emporium. It should have been a happy year for the partners, but no one could have predicted the tragedy to come.

Like Pirie, Carson had also been spending a great deal of time in New York. He and Betsey split their time between Chicago and Brooklyn, while MacLeish and the Scott brothers handled the day-to-day operations on State Street. For quite a while, however, Samuel hadn't been well. His appetite was off, and he grew gaunt and feverish. A persistent hacking cough dogged him throughout the day, and drenching sweats tortured him at night. On Monday, September 13, 1869, Sam Carson succumbed to the ravages of tuberculosis—then known as consumption—at his residence in Brooklyn. He was only forty-one years old. Sadly, just two short years later, almost to the day, his dear wife, Elizabeth Pirie Carson, followed him to the grave. Although little has been recorded about the cause of her death, she passed away in 1871 at the age of forty and was buried at the Moorestown Baptist Churchyard in Burlington County, New Jersey. There is also a monument in memory of Elizabeth; her mother, Mary; and other relatives at St. Patrick Church of Ireland graveyard in Newry.

The deaths were a devastating blow to John Pirie. Sometimes business dealings can strain friendships, but that wasn't the case between Carson and Pirie; the two remained exceptionally close throughout their association. To lose his best friend and then his sister in such a short time seemed the ultimate cruelty. Pirie vowed that they would not be forgotten. He swore that for as long as he lived, the business would retain the name of Carson and Pirie as a tribute to his partner and best mate. Amazingly, nearly a century and a half after Carson's untimely death, the company still bears his name. Unfortunately, Pirie would have little time to mourn before fate dealt him another misfortune.

Chapter 3

THE GREAT CONFLAGRATION

You can scarcely imagine the desolation. If a man wants his mind impressed with
what the end of the world will be, let him come here.
—James W. Milner, eyewitness

In October 1871, Chicago was suffering through the effects of a lingering drought that had parched the city for months. Only a scant two and a half inches of rain had fallen since July, a mere trifle compared to the usual average of about fourteen inches for that stretch of time. The normally muddy streets were bone dry, with wagon ruts and hoof prints captured in stark relief in the hardened, chalky soil. As carriages clattered across the furrows, fine clouds of dust and grit swirled in their wake, forming miniature vortexes that danced across the barren streets. The hot, relentless southwest winds scattered dried leaves, twigs and debris that crackled loudly underfoot, and small fires leapt up with alarming frequency.

In fact, for most of that autumn, the air had hardly been fit to breathe. An acrid haze of smoke from smoldering prairie fires hung over the city like a shroud, causing pedestrians to clamp handkerchiefs over their noses and mouths in a vain attempt to fend off the choking, stinging fog. But Chicago wasn't alone in its misery; the entire Midwest was dry as tinder. One observer noted that the atmosphere itself seemed altered, as if all the moisture had been wrung out and replaced with an odd sort of static electricity. Not surprisingly, the constant fires were taking a toll on the Chicago Fire Department. They would barely put out one, and yet another would flare up as if to taunt them. There had been twenty significant fires in the first week of October alone. Both men and equipment were strained to the limit.

On Saturday, October 7, a massive blaze consumed a lumberyard and sawmill on South Canal Street. It took more than seventeen hours to extinguish, and in the process, a hook and ladder truck, several hoses and various other pieces of equipment were destroyed. In addition, the coal needed to stoke the pumping steamers was running in short supply. The firefighters were eventually triumphant but exhausted by the epic battle. Little did they know that inferno was just a preview of the hellish fire to come.

Sunday, October 8, dawned unseasonably warm and hazy. It was a typical fall day, filled with church and chores and family gatherings for most residents. Patrick and Catherine O'Leary, Irish immigrants who lived at 137 De Koven Street on the southwest side of the city, were no different. After a busy day, Catherine tucked the couple's five children into their beds, and she and Patrick retired shortly thereafter at about 8:30 p.m. The O'Leary homestead included two modest cottages and a barn where Catherine kept milking cows and a horse and wagon that she used to supplement Patrick's laborer wages. The O'Learys lived in the rear cottage near the barn, and they rented the front cottage to the McLaughlin family. That evening, the McLaughlins were having a party, and Catherine drifted off to sleep to the sound of fiddle music and laughter emanating from the neighboring home.

At about 9:00 p.m., the O'Learys were startled awake by the sound of pounding and shouting at their front door. It was another neighbor, Daniel "Peg Leg" Sullivan—so named because of his wooden leg—yelling "Fire! Fire!" They scrambled from bed and raced outside to see their barn enveloped in flames. Daniel gasped that he had tried to rescue the animals, but he had only been able to save one young calf before being beaten back by the flames. Catherine's five cows and a horse perished in the blaze. Although it was too late to save the barn, the neighbors and partygoers immediately formed a bucket brigade and began to pour water on the cottages to prevent the fire from spreading, while another man ran down the block to pull a fire alarm. Unfortunately, in an effort to prevent false alarms, the fire call boxes of that time required a key that was held by a nearby merchant or resident, and no one could find the key holder for the closest box. In desperation, the man continued to run until he found an attended call box at a pharmacy some distance away, where the alarm was finally sounded, but there is some evidence that the signal never reached the fire dispatcher.

At about the same time, a fire-spotter at the downtown courthouse observed the telltale red glow of flames to the southwest and rang the alarm.

His perception of distance, however, was sadly off, and he sent firefighters scrambling about a mile distant from the actual fire. By the time the location was finally sorted out, almost an hour had passed, and the little barn fire was now a monster raging out of control. The nearly gale-force winds that night whipped the flames into a frenzy and sent burning embers scampering across the wooden rooftops to the north and east. At first, firefighters held out hope that the fire would die out when it reached the south branch of the Chicago River, but the inferno roared across the wharf, burning moored boats and hopscotching easily across the water to the east. Some witnesses claimed that the oily foul river itself combusted, with tongues of flame shimmering across the surface. As the blaze marched unabated toward the city center, its blowing embers ignited other areas until an estimated total of nine separate tornadoes of fire crawled across the land. By midnight, it was heading straight for the heart of the city.

At about 2:00 a.m., Andrew MacLeish was sleeping peacefully at his residence on Ada Street on the northwest side of the city when he was awakened by a pounding at the door. It was his brother-in-law, James Chalmers, who had heard of a massive fire that was threatening the commercial district. It was so serious that Chalmers's neighbor had been summoned by messenger to make his way downtown and attempt to rescue the account books of his employer. MacLeish hastily dressed, hitched up his horse to its buggy and raced for George Scott's home on Randolph Street. After awakening Scott and quickly apprising him of the situation, the two men rushed toward their State Street business. The scene that greeted them as they approached the city was one of chaos and horror; it seemed as if the whole land was ablaze, as surging mobs fought to escape the flames. The bridges across the river at Madison, Randolph and Lake were each impassable. MacLeish steered the carriage to the north, toward the crossing at Kinzie Street, but fire was already licking at that bridge, and the authorities waved them away.

In frustration, MacLeish wheeled his horse first westward and then south toward Twelfth Street in a long and circuitous route around the inferno. By the time they reached State Street, the fire was advancing quickly and they had little time to act. Scott hurriedly gathered important company books and papers, while MacLeish desperately bargained with wagon drivers and hacks in an attempt to save some merchandise. In spite of their efforts, only a small amount of inventory was actually moved to safety before they were forced to retreat from the flames. MacLeish later recalled:

The Great Chicago Fire of 1871 left the city in ashes.

Mr. Scott and myself made our way southward on the streets [yet] untouched by the fire, after first seeing our own premises enveloped in the great conflagration… When I reached home, sometime in the afternoon, and saw in a mirror my appearance, with my face blackened and unrecognizable, I remember giving way to the feelings called forth by this stupendous and awful calamity.

By the early hours of Monday morning, the flames had jumped the main branch of the Chicago River and reached the waterworks on the north side. Once the water supply was cut off, there was no means left to fight the firestorm, and the city was completely at its mercy. It continued to burn its way northward, wiping out a large swath of residential property and leaving thousands homeless before it slowly began to run out of fuel. On Tuesday,

October 10, a light but steady rain finally extinguished the stubborn flames, but there was little left to save. In the end, the great fire killed more than 300 people and burned four square miles of the city in a path of destruction that stretched for thirty-four city blocks. Final damage estimates exceeded $220 million, about one-third of the city's entire valuation. Tragically, at least 100,000 people—a full one-third of the population—were left homeless, many with just the clothes on their backs. Naysayers believed that the city could not possibly recover from such a deadly blow, but Chicago had nothing if not spirit. The embers had barely cooled before residents and business owners began to plan the massive rebuilding.

In fact, the day after the fire, a group of the city's top merchants and real estate developers met at a private club to discuss their options. Although most businesses had at least some insurance, the disaster was of such magnitude that several insurance companies ultimately foundered, leaving the policy holders with little recourse. The cost of rebuilding would be enormous. Potter Palmer, Marshall Field, Levi Leiter, George Scott and many others gathered to exchange ideas. A few of the men in attendance felt that the city was beyond hope, and they debated repudiating their debts and leaving town. Field would have none of that, however, and announced that his firm would reopen immediately. Pirie, Scott and MacLeish agreed, and the others soon followed suit. Within a few weeks, Field and Leiter opened a temporary retail store in a remodeled horse barn that was still standing at State and Twentieth Streets, and shortly thereafter, Scott secured a five-story brick building at Madison and Franklin that would serve as the new quarters for Carson and Pirie's wholesale business. And, in perhaps the ultimate display of bravado, Potter Palmer announced that he would begin construction at once on a new and improved Palmer House Hotel to replace the breathtaking original, which had fallen to the flames just thirteen days after its magnificent grand opening. This time, he boasted, the new inn would be fireproof, and he dared anyone to prove him wrong. In an advertisement for the reincarnated hotel, he challenged curiosity seekers and aspiring arsonists to attempt to set the hotel ablaze: "If at the expiration of [one hour], the fire does not spread beyond the room, the person accepting this invitation is to pay for all damages done and for the use of the room. If the fire does extend beyond the room (I claim it will not), there shall be no charge for the damage done."

The cause of the great fire has never been established, but there are plenty of theories. Perhaps the most enduring—but totally incorrect—explanation is that Catherine O'Leary went out to milk a cow, and the cantankerous animal kicked over a lantern, starting the barn aflame. This legend was repeated in songs, poems and movies and resulted in Mrs. O'Leary's vilification and abuse. She was threatened, harassed and portrayed as a vile, alcoholic old hag. In reality, she was a hardworking and sober young mother and was completely innocent of the charges leveled against her. Michael Ahern, a reporter for the *Chicago Tribune*, first broadcast the "cow theory" in an article the day after the fire but finally retracted the charges a few decades later and admitted it was all a fabrication. It was no doubt fueled by the anti-Irish sentiment that was prevalent at the time, and Ahern said that he felt it would make "colorful copy." Sadly, the O'Leary family lived under a cloud of suspicion for the rest of their lives.

Investigations immediately after the fire cast suspicion on Daniel Sullivan, the neighbor who awoke the sleeping family. There were numerous inconsistencies in his recollections of the fateful night, and detectives believed that he might have started the blaze by accident, perhaps by careless use of smoking materials, and then panicked and tried to cover up his involvement. Years later, another neighbor, Louis Cohn, claimed responsibility for the fire, saying that he knocked over a lantern during a covert craps game being played in the barn. He later recanted, however, and little evidence was found to support his story.

Perhaps the most intriguing theory is that the fire was caused by fragments of Biela's Comet that rained meteorites across the Great Lakes region that night. Many scientists scoff at the idea, primarily because meteorites that do survive our atmosphere are cool to the touch by the time they strike earth. However, the odd pattern of fires that ringed Lakes Michigan and Huron that October evening lends some credence to the notion. In Peshtigo, Wisconsin, a raging tornado of fire killed more than two thousand people at the same time as Chicago burned to the south, and similar but less deadly fires also struck the Michigan cities of Port Huron, Manistee and Holland that night. Interestingly, some survivors at Peshtigo reported seeing "balls of fire" and "blue flames" falling from the sky just before the conflagration. Burning methane gas produces blue flames, and methane is a characteristic byproduct of meteorites, which decompose and produce the gas as they pass through the atmosphere. Sadly, the tragic loss of life and property in the Wisconsin and Michigan fires was barely noted in the U.S. and international press, which focused almost entirely on the dramatic scene in Chicago.

Although it would be years before the city recovered completely, the new buildings that sprang up after the fire were generally taller, grander, safer and featured modern conveniences such as steam elevators. By 1873, Field

After the fire, new buildings grew taller and safer, with steel replacing wood for construction.

and Leiter were back on their corner at State and Washington, ensconced in a beautiful new building built by the Singer Sewing Machine Company. Carson, Pirie and Company, while flourishing in its wholesale location at Madison and Franklin, had not yet found a permanent site for retail. The company opened a store on Twenty-second Street, but it was far removed from the hustle and bustle of State Street. Shortly after, it launched a second store on West Madison but soon consolidated both locations into a larger building at Madison and Peoria on the west side. Still not satisfied, MacLeish rented a storefront at Clark and Erie in 1876 to give the company a north side location.

Despite the optimism that defined Chicago at the time, the post-fire years brought economic hardship and uncertainty. The ripples of a financial crisis that began in Europe soon reached U.S. shores and culminated in a severe economic depression that came to be known as the Panic of 1873. In September of that year, financier Jay Cooke and Company, long regarded as one of the strongest financial institutions in the United States, suddenly closed its doors after being squeezed by inflation and railroad speculation. Almost immediately, other banks across the nation began to fail, five in Chicago alone. Stocks dropped so precipitously that the New York Stock Exchange closed for ten days that month in an attempt to quell the panic. By November, approximately fifty-five railroads had gone bankrupt, and another sixty failed within the following year. The value of merchandise tumbled, and many merchants found themselves with warehouses full of goods that were valued at less than they had originally paid.

Through it all, Chicago suffered a bit less than the rest of the country, due in part to the massive rebuilding of the burnt city, which created jobs and buffered the local economy. Still, times were tough, and some businesses couldn't survive. Many of the city's smaller dry goods retailers and wholesalers disappeared, but those that were able to ride out the storm came through stronger, smarter and with less competition. That was certainly the case for Carson, Pirie and Company. Near the end of the decade, sales were strong, but the firm hadn't yet found a better location for its retail business.

Meanwhile, Pirie's competitors Field and Leiter faced another calamity. On November 14, 1877, yet another fire struck, roaring through its store at State and Washington, completely gutting the beautiful new building and destroying millions of dollars in inventory. To make matters worse, the Christmas buying season—the most critical and profitable time for retailers—was just beginning. Field, however, was not a man to be deterred. He immediately rented the Inter-State Industrial Palace, a massive exhibition building perched on Chicago's lakefront, and filled it with inventory from his wholesale division. Less than two weeks later, Field and Leiter opened its temporary store just in time for the Christmas crowds. It was an unlikely location for retail, set far from the downtown commercial district and situated forlornly on the frozen Lake Michigan shoreline. To mitigate some of the accessibility issues, Field arranged an expensive omnibus service to pick up shoppers at the corner of State and Randolph every five minutes and deposit them directly at the exhibition hall's front door. It wasn't an ideal situation, but it would have to suffice for a while.

After the fire, the Singer Company wasted no time in rebuilding at the corner of State and Washington. Once again, a new marble palace began to rise from the ashes. During the reconstruction, it was always assumed that Field and Leiter would return to the rebuilt store, and that suited Field just fine. Except this time, he wanted to buy the building instead of renting. Singer officials were more than willing to consider an outright sale and arranged a meeting. At the time, Field was away on a buying trip, so Leiter attended the discussions alone. Unfortunately, the short-tempered and often unreasonable Leiter immediately angered the Singer representatives and shut down the negotiations when they named what he considered to be an exorbitant amount. The asking price was $700,000. Leiter fumed that he would not pay a penny more than $500,000 and shouted, "If we don't take the building, you won't find another tenant in Chicago for it!" Leiter was wrong—they could and they did, promptly leasing the space to Carson, Pirie and Company for $700,000 per year.

When word reached Field about what had transpired, he was absolutely livid. Not only had Leiter thoughtlessly tossed away their premium location on State Street, but he had allowed it to fall into the hands of their biggest competitor. Field rushed back to Chicago to salvage the situation, but with no bargaining power left, he was forced to agree to the full asking price of $700,000. Even worse, he now owned a beautiful building that was soon to be occupied by his competition! Pirie, Scott and MacLeish were well aware of the awkward position into which this placed Field, and they weren't about to make it easy on him. The clever Scots agreed to forfeit their lease if the price was right; it would cost Field another $100,000 in cash to obtain their cooperation. He reluctantly paid, and for the rest of his life he referred to Carson, Pirie and Company as "the three Scotsmen" with a mixture of derision and grudging respect.

Although they had walked away from the deal with a hefty bonus, they were now back to square one in their search for a new retail location.

In February 1883, Charles Gossage—a dry goods merchant who was a minor competitor of Pirie's—passed away, and his family offered to sell the company. Pirie was perhaps more interested in the firm's location at State and Washington than he was in its trade, but in any case he agreed to purchase the business for $1 million. It continued to operate under the Gossage name until 1890, when it was greatly expanded and remodeled and both of Carson's existing retail stores were closed and consolidated into that location.

By 1891, combined wholesale and retail sales reached nearly $20 million. Although the firm now employed almost two thousand workers, it was still in many ways a family business. Pirie's sons, Carson's nephews and several members of the large Scott family ran the day-to-day business along with MacLeish and his son, while Pirie tended to the finances and the foreign buying offices from his home in New York. John Scott, the son of George Scott, had become such a valuable asset that he was brought in as a partner, and the company name was officially changed to Carson Pirie Scott and Company, the name that would continue to identify the stores for more than 120 years into the future. And yet, in many ways, growth was just beginning.

Chapter 4
SULLIVAN'S VISION

An architect, to be a true exponent of his time, must possess first, last and always the sympathy, the intuition of a poet…this is the one real, vital principle that survives through all places and all times.
—Louis Henri Sullivan, American architect

Immediately following Chicago's Great Fire, the once-thriving commercial landscape was a vast desert of rubble and heartbreak. Although the city harbored lofty plans to rebuild, many merchants simply faded away, either unable or unwilling to begin again. Those who were determined to stay were forced into temporary quarters far removed from the charred ruins of State Street, Potter Palmer's grand boulevard of commerce. Yet although the future was murky, it was also charged with endless possibilities—a blank canvas for those who possessed the spirit, vision and capital to create the next chapter in Chicago's history. It was, in short, an entrepreneur's dream. And for two young German immigrants, it was the perfect time to finally realize those dreams.

Actually, it's impossible to tell the story of Carson Pirie Scott without first telling the story of Schlesinger and Mayer. Leopold Schlesinger was born in Brotchizen, Germany, in 1842. His family was modestly wealthy, and young Leopold enjoyed the advantages of an extensive education. After he completed his university studies, he traveled to Chicago in 1862 to seek his fortune. He began his career as an office clerk for a small dry goods wholesaler, where he carefully studied the trade and judiciously put away a portion of his earnings, in the hope that someday he could develop his own firm. It was during this time that he met and became fast friends with another young German named David Mayer.

Like Leopold, David had been born in Germany, but his family immigrated to America in early 1852, while David was still an infant. The Mayers weren't quite as prosperous as the Schlesingers, and as a child, David attended public school in Chicago. By his early teens, he quit school in favor of work. What he lacked in formal education, however, he more than made up for with a strong work ethic, a sharp intelligence and the ability to inspire trust and loyalty. Together, the two men pooled their resources and in February 1872 opened a small dry goods shop at the corner of Madison and DesPlaines Streets on the west side, in what was once the St. Denis Hotel. At the time, Madison Street was the major east–west route for the horse-car lines, and some thought that it would assume the position that State Street had held before the fire. Business was good for the young men, and they soon opened a second branch farther west on Madison at Peoria Street. The business of Schlesinger and Mayer was positioned to appeal to the middle-class trade, much the same as Carson Pirie Scott. Their merchandise was not quite as upscale as that offered by Field and Leiter but well above the common goods offered by low-priced merchants of the day such as The Fair Store or the Beehive.

Trade positioning, it seems, wasn't the only similarity between Schlesinger and Mayer and Carson and Pirie; in 1873, Leopold married Henrietta Mayer, who was David's sister. David did not continue the trend, however, and remained a bachelor for two decades until he married Florence Blum of New York in 1893. By all accounts, the men's partnership was successful and pleasant. They shared many interests, including memberships in the exclusive private Union League Club and the Standard Club of Chicago. Both organizations were founded in the mid- to late 1800s to promote civic, social and philanthropic interests, and they each contributed greatly to Chicago's cultural and community development. Both Schlesinger and Mayer were active members and gave generously of their resources. In fact, Mayer later attributed their business success to a policy of honest dealings and civic responsibility.

But despite the early success of their west side stores, it was becoming apparent that State Street was slowly regaining its prominence as the city's commercial hub. Field's and Carson's had returned, and other merchants were gradually filling in along the rebuilt street. If Schlesinger and Mayer wanted to remain competitive, they would need to find a suitable location to grow their firm. In April 1881, they signed a lease for a portion of the ground-floor space of the Bowen Building on the southeast corner of State and Madison. It was an ideal spot; the commanding and beautiful Parisian-style façade of the building boldly dominated the intersection and created an image of a fashionable cosmopolitan emporium. This new positioning allowed them to attract a portion of the well-to-do carriage trade from Marshall Field and Company—newly renamed after Levi Leiter's retirement—and yet their merchandise selection and average price points weren't too far out of reach for some of the more bargain-minded shoppers who typically patronized The Fair. In fact, the Bowen Building's site was almost equidistant from Field's to the north and The Fair to the south.

Another advantage to the new location was that it sat squarely at the crossroads of the fancy new cable car system that was slowly replacing the old horse-drawn cars. Operated by the Chicago City Railway, the line opened on January 28, 1882, and was just the second cable car line in the country after the famed San Francisco system. Although some naysayers doubted the technology would work in Chicago's frigid climate, it turned out to be surprisingly reliable. It employed a continuously moving loop of heavy cable that ran just below street grade and traced a path from State and Madison east to Wabash Avenue, north to Lake Street, west back to State and south to Thirty-ninth Street. The route was also shared with the Wabash/Cottage Grove line, which continued south and east to Fifty-fifth Street. Later, the service was expanded to many other parts of the city, but it's likely that this original rectangular course of cable spawned Chicago's long-standing nickname for its downtown business district: the Loop.

The new cable cars were a merchant's dream, at least for those whose businesses stood along the route. No matter what the weather, they delivered a steady stream of shoppers right to the doors of Carson's, Field's and Schlesinger and Mayer. All the businesses profited, but the Schlesinger and Mayer store enjoyed the most prominent location at the junction of the system. This distinction, however, didn't come without a price. In fact, its corner was considered some of the most costly real estate in all of Chicago, with a price of $3,000 per frontage foot by 1890. To remain profitable, it needed to continue expanding in order to generate sufficient revenue to keep pace with the escalating real estate prices. It was no surprise, then, that it quickly stretched beyond its original floor plan. At first, it expanded upward by leasing floors from its upstairs neighbor, wholesaler Clement, Moore and Company. Soon it occupied the entire building and began to acquire additional storefronts adjacent to the Bowen Building to the south on State. As the store grew, the partners commenced a series of remodeling projects in an attempt to give

Harry Gordon Selfridge bought the Sullivan Building but quickly sold it to Carson Pirie Scott.

the new additions a unified appearance. By 1890, they had expanded farther down State, and they knew it was time to move beyond their patchwork approach. This time, they would spare no expense and perform a dramatic renovation. And, of course, they would hire the best to achieve that goal: none other than Dankmar Adler and Louis Sullivan.

The architectural firm of Adler and Sullivan designed more than 250 buildings during its fifteen-year partnership, employing a style that was both distinctly American and highly functional. In fact, Sullivan's personal mantra was "form ever follows function," and that philosophy was perhaps best expressed in Chicago's Auditorium Building, the crowning jewel of their long collaboration. The multipurpose building—which still stands today at the corner of Michigan Avenue and Congress Parkway—was completed in 1889 and houses a world-class theater with seating for 4,200, perfect acoustics and breathtaking design. An 1890 addition added a 400-room hotel (which now houses Roosevelt University) and 136 office suites. The partners' talents meshed perfectly; Adler was a gifted engineer as well as an architect, and he was responsible for the theater's acoustics, its innovative raft foundation that allowed the massive structure to be built on soft clay and the auditorium's central air-conditioning system, which made it one of the first public buildings in the country to enjoy such a novelty. Sullivan, on the other hand, was the firm's visual master. An artiste in both talent and disposition, he was an avid student of the writings of Walt Whitman and Henry David Thoreau. He incorporated themes of nature into the ornamentation of many of his buildings, such as intricate scrollwork of vines, leaves and other organic elements that he used to draw the eye upward and enhance the perception of a building's height.

Although Adler and Sullivan created magic in their tall buildings, their personal lives were quite another matter. Adler was short, portly and genial, well liked and respected by both his clients and the many draftsmen under his employ. Frank Lloyd Wright, a young apprentice of the firm who would later go on to achieve his own considerable fame, described him as a kind and fatherly man who took great interest in his associates' work. He was known to roll up his rumpled shirtsleeves and perch on the edge of a drafting stool, offering advice and encouragement. Adler and his wife had three children (two sons and a daughter), whom he apparently doted on, as well as a wide circle of friends. By contrast, Sullivan was tall, thin and insular—some would say arrogant—and had little use for his underlings. Although he considered Wright a friend and would sometimes engage him in long philosophical conversations in the quiet at the end of a busy day, Wright recalled that the other draftsmen "might as well have been office furniture" in Sullivan's eyes. Although Sullivan did wed Mary Azona Hattabaugh, the couple separated after some years. He had no children and, it seems, few close friends. By most accounts, Sullivan sought solace in the bottle, struggling with a lifelong addiction to alcohol. Many clients found him difficult and temperamental. David Mayer, however, had a great respect for the brooding architect's talent and knew that he and Adler would be the perfect team to renovate Schlesinger and Mayer's beautiful but cramped store at State and Madison.

Adler and Sullivan faced the challenge of increasing the square footage without losing the structure's imposing and distinctive façade. They sacrificed the building's original ornamental corner dome and mansard roof to add two additional stories and topped the now-flat roof with an ornate cornice of cast iron. The dramatically embellished ironwork was painted a brilliant white, and the architects carried the design through the new storefront acquisitions on State, effectively creating the appearance of one large, sleek building. The beautiful curved front of the Bowen Building remained, commanding attention from any passersby and drawing attention to the large display windows that flanked the intersection.

In 1893, however, the nation once again slipped into a deep financial crisis. It began in part due to a sudden halt in investments by a large Argentinean bank, which caused a run on gold in the U.S. Treasury. The waves of panic spread throughout parts of Europe, and some foreign investors began to rapidly sell off American stocks. Eventually, nearly six hundred banks across the country failed, several railroads shut down and approximately fifteen thousand businesses shuttered their doors. Unemployment was rampant; one oft-quoted source estimated that, on average, eighteen out of every one hundred people were out of work by 1894, but many areas were hit much harder. New York was said to reach a peak of 35 percent unemployment that year, and in parts of Michigan, a heartbreaking 43 percent of the population was hungry and jobless. Although Chicago was once again spared the worst of it, the city was not unaffected.

Schlesinger and Mayer enjoyed a steady, if somewhat reduced, stream of business. Their architects, however, were not so lucky. The poor economy led to fewer commissions, and although Adler borrowed money to keep the firm afloat for a while, in 1895, Adler and Sullivan dissolved their partnership. Adler briefly accepted a position with the Crane Elevator Company but soon realized his heart was in architecture, and he eventually opened a new practice with his sons. Sullivan struggled to build a solo practice but had some difficulty attracting clients. Frank Lloyd Wright—who had himself been fired by Sullivan in 1893 following an acrimonious dispute over Wright's moonlighting as a residential architect—observed that the client base of Adler and Sullivan had been overwhelmingly loyal to Adler. Only a handful remained with Sullivan after the split, but David Mayer was one of them.

In spite of the economy, Schlesinger and Mayer continued to grow their business. In 1896, they purchased a four-story stone-fronted building on Wabash Avenue that backed up against their State Street holdings. The partners knew that the Union Elevated Railroad would soon open an elevated commuter railroad along the avenue, and competitors Marshall Field and Mandel Brothers had already begun to expand eastward to Wabash in response to the limited and expensive footage along State. Mayer retained Sullivan to redesign the building and create an elegant east entrance for the expected throngs of commuters who would transit through the Wabash and Madison station each day.

In the initial stage of the project, Sullivan opened up the façade on the building's first two floors, creating massive plate-glass display windows framed by intricate iron scrollwork. The next phase included plans to add six more stories to the original structure, thus creating a commanding ten-story edifice, but for some reason this was never carried out. Instead, Sullivan designed and built a stunning pedestrian bridge that spanned the street from the elevated station to the second-floor entrance of the new Wabash addition. The ornamented steel-girded passage was enclosed with floor-to-ceiling plate glass, which protected shoppers from inclement weather yet allowed them a bird's-eye view of the street below. The roof was a continuous skylight, and electric lights throughout the passageway cast a warm glow

An early postcard depicts the Carson's store at State and Madison.

that drew shoppers into the welcoming doors of the store. From street level, its appearance belied its strength; it looked to be an elegant corridor of glass suspended by a delicate lacework of ornamental iron. Not surprisingly, it was soon dubbed "the crystal bridge."

In many ways, the merchants of that era defined themselves—and created an aura of success and desirability—through their architecture. The competition to remain fresh and relevant in the public's eye resulted in an almost-constant reinvention of each merchant's physical location. As soon as one store remodeled or added additional sales space, it created a ripple effect down the length of State Street. Thus, when Mandel Brothers began an extensive renovation directly across the street from Schlesinger and Mayer, the partners knew that they had to rethink their plans in order to compete. Perhaps it was time to begin anew. And so, in 1898, Schlesinger met with their landlord, Levi Leiter, to discuss the possibility of a brand-new building. Leiter had retired from his partnership with Marshall Field in 1881 and turned his attention to real estate, and he soon acquired a portfolio of desirable properties, including the site at Madison and State. Typically, merchants leased the land and buildings that contained their stores, but the expense of any new construction fell to the lessee. Having a tenant that was willing to shoulder the cost for a new and improved structure was obviously attractive to Leiter. He agreed to an extended lease and gave Schlesinger and Mayer permission to construct a new building, with a few caveats. The facility had to be at least eight stories tall, completely fireproof and of steel and iron construction. Leiter also reserved the right to approve the final plans. Sullivan was once again offered the commission, and he immediately headed for the drafting table.

His initial proposal was for a twelve-story steel-framed structure to be finished with a façade of marble and bronze. It was an ambitious project with an estimated cost of $1 million, leaving some critics skeptical about whether it would truly come to fruition. Sullivan would also be briefly reunited with his old partner Adler, who accepted the position of mechanical engineer to design the building's power plant. But before the construction even began, Levi Leiter suffered some financial reversals and was forced to sell the property to Marshall Field, whose own fabulously successful store sat just one block to the north. Field, however, had a long-standing belief that competition was healthy and necessary, and to Schlesinger and Mayer's great relief, he quickly agreed to allow the project to proceed. In 1899, work began on a section of Madison Street. The original plans had been revised several times to conform to the city's height restrictions and other building constraints, and the design now called for a nine-story edifice. The construction was scheduled in stages so that the store could continue to operate and generate much-needed revenue, and by early December 1899, the Madison Street section had opened its doors to hordes of Christmas shoppers eager for a look at the luxurious and modern facility. The development had been costly though, and the partners needed some time to recoup before they could begin the next phase.

The venture languished until 1902, when Henry Siegel of Siegel, Cooper and Company offered to buy into the partnership. By this time, Schlesinger was worn out from the many years of hard work and decided to retire. He sold his half of the partnership to Siegel, who came aboard as vice-president and chief investor. David Mayer assumed the role of president, and all parties agreed to retain the firm's well-established name of Schlesinger and Mayer. But now, with Siegel's infusion of capital, the planned rebuilding could proceed. By this time, the city council had relaxed height restrictions, and the new partners proceeded with Sullivan's original twelve-story plan for the State Street side. In order to disrupt trade as little as possible, the construction firm of George Fuller and Company devised a method of shoring up the original Bowen Building and sinking a new foundation beneath it while business in the store continued as usual. Only after the

Left: The ornate rotunda entrance creates a dramatic presence on Chicago's busiest corner.

Below: Louis Sullivan's distinctive iron scrollwork incorporated elements of nature. His stylized initials "LS" are visible to the right of the arch. *Photo by Peter Rimsa.*

foundation was complete and the Christmas shopping season was behind them in January 1903 did they begin demolition of the old building.

The finished structure, which was completed in the fall of 1903, featured a rounded entrance with arched doorways embellished with elaborate iron scrollwork that continued across the first two floors. Glossy ivory enameled ornamental terra cotta climbed the exterior walls and flanked the wide windows that let sunlight stream far into the interior. The beautiful edifice was reminiscent of an exclusive Parisian department store, Magasins du Printemps, and it brought an air of elegance to the corner that was unlike any of its peers along State Street. Unfortunately, it also came at an astronomical price; the price of building alone had exceeded $1.6 million due to serious cost overruns, and more interior work was required. The inevitable temporary decrease in sales due to construction had seriously hurt the firm, and Mayer was struggling with a heavy debt load. He had first approached his new partner, Henry Siegel, for additional funding in early 1903 while the work was still in progress, but Siegel was reluctant to invest any more.

Mayer also tried to strike an agreement with Otto Young, who owned the land parcels south of the new store. Mayer envisioned a huge building complex that filled the entire block, but after much negotiation, the deal fell apart. Some say it was because Young would not agree to use Sullivan as an architect and Mayer refused to be disloyal to Sullivan by turning the work over to Daniel Burnham, Young's preferred architect. In any case, the relationship between the two men turned quite acrimonious, and any future chances for expansion seemed unlikely. Mayer was dead tired of the struggle and perhaps more than a little overwhelmed. He had to find a better solution.

While all this drama was unfolding down the street, Carson Pirie Scott was facing its own problems. Although business was quite good, the company had been informed that its soon-to-expire lease for its retail store in the Reliance Building at Washington and State would not be renewed, since the building would be sold to the Hillman's grocery company. Losing a presence on State Street was not an option; the partners knew they needed to find a new location quickly, but available square footage was scarce, especially for a store of such grand size. David Mayer knew of their predicament and thought maybe he had the perfect solution. In March 1903, he approached Pirie with a proposal: the two stores could merge at Mayer's beautiful new building, perhaps operating under the name of Carson, Pirie and Mayer. It was a fascinating offer but quite a drastic step. Pirie, Scott and MacLeish would need some time to consider their options. Mayer, however, was impatient and exhausted. While the Scotsmen were mulling it over, he would continue to cast around for a solution. Little did anyone know that a third player was about to enter the picture and completely change the dynamics.

Across the street from Carson's, Marshall Field still reigned as the undisputed merchant king. Field had an uncanny ability for uncovering and promoting talent from within his organization, and one of those rising stars was a young man named Harry Gordon Selfridge. A Wisconsin native, Selfridge had moved to Chicago from Jackson, Michigan, and began work in 1879 with Field as a ten-dollar-a-week stock boy. Harry was exuberant, dramatic and hurried. He soon gained the nickname "mile-a-minute Harry" for his breathless speech and rapid gait. Some considered him brash and vulgar, but Field recognized him as a man with vision and an unerring instinct for what the customer wanted. He quickly moved through the ranks to a position as head of the entire retail division, and in 1891, he was awarded a 2/85 partnership share in the firm, with Field loaning him the $200,000 in required capital. In spite of this success, Selfridge wanted more. He was chafing at his rivalry with John Shedd, another partner in the firm who appeared to be Field's heir apparent. Selfridge wanted his own store where he could put forth his ideas without any interference or input from anyone else. And so, in his typical impetuous style, he marched into "the old boss man's office" and announced that he was leaving to go into business for himself. Mr. Field, who was perhaps not particularly surprised, said very little other than to wish him good luck.

Selfridge quickly traded his partnership interest in Field's for $1.5 million and approached David Mayer with a proposal. His timing was perfect; Mayer was more than happy to get out, and he promptly sold the entire interest in the firm of Schlesinger and Mayer for a reported sum of $5 million. "Mile-a-minute Harry" had the beginnings of his own empire. But no sooner than the ink had dried on the contract, Selfridge realized that he was in deeply over his head. He really didn't have sufficient capital to run the business. Almost immediately, he discussed a deal with Otto Young, Mayer's old nemesis, to sell the building and leaseholds to Young and simply lease back the property. The plan would work out well for all involved; Mayer had retired with a sizeable fortune, Young would own most or all of the buildings on the east side of State between Madison and Monroe and Selfridge possessed a beautiful, elegant department store. Everyone was happy. Or, at least, almost everyone. After just a few months of operating the new store, Selfridge wanted out. He loudly complained that the employees lacked the same work ethic and enthusiasm as those he had employed at Field's, and he quickly found himself overwhelmed and with no one qualified to offer support. "There are a million things to do and nobody to do them!" he grumbled. And so, in desperation, he sheepishly turned to his old rival at Field's, John Shedd, for help and advice.

The next morning, as Shedd pondered the situation, he bumped into John T. Pirie in front of the Field's store. Pirie apologetically admitted that he had been snooping about Field's latest window displays, and with an embarrassed nod, he turned to go. Suddenly, Shedd realized that there was a simple solution to everyone's dilemma. He eagerly pleaded with Pirie to come up to his office for a discussion. Pirie at first was reluctant, but Shedd soon convinced him that there was an urgent opportunity at hand. It was common knowledge on the street that Carson Pirie Scott was desperately seeking new quarters, and with his private awareness of Selfridge's desire to quit the business, he believed he could help broker a deal that would solve both men's problems.

Pirie initially scoffed at the idea. After all, Selfridge had been in business for a scant few months, and it seemed ludicrous that he would already be willing to sell. The whole concept seemed like a colossal waste of time and energy. But Pirie knew that John Shedd was a man of honor and integrity, and it appeared as though he had some insight in the matter. Shedd offered to orchestrate the negotiations, acting strictly as a neutral friend to both parties. Pirie was intrigued and finally agreed to proceed with talks. Shedd picked up the telephone and made arrangements for Selfridge to meet them immediately at the offices of the Illinois Trust Safe Deposit Company. Pirie contacted his son, Samuel Carson Pirie, who was running most of the day-to-day operations of the firm, and asked him to join them.

When they arrived at the bank a short time later, Shedd quickly procured three consultation rooms; he occupied the center room, with Selfridge in the room on the right and the Piries to the left. Within half an hour, the first offer was made; Selfridge would sell the entire business for the $5 million he had paid plus a $250,000 bonus. The Piries countered with an offer of $5 million plus a $150,000 bonus. Shedd dashed from room to room with scraps of paper containing scribbled notes, questions and bids. After a brief flurry of negotiation, they reached a compromise: $5 million plus a $200,000 bonus. Sam C. Pirie accepted by jotting "Sold, S.C.P." on the latest paper scrap, and Shedd signed with Selfridge's authority "O.K. Selfridge." When the men gathered to shake hands, Selfridge voiced one concern; although nothing had been signed, he was in the middle of negotiations with Otto Young regarding the sale and leaseback of the property. He feared the possibility

The Sullivan Building, including the breathtaking façade, was completely restored in 2007. *Photo by Peter Rimsa.*

that Young might try to enforce their verbal agreement, so he added a caveat to the scrap paper: "O.K. if Young agrees."

The next morning, Otto Young agreed to relinquish any claims, but the Piries weren't having such an easy time of it. The many partners of Carson Pirie Scott felt that Sam Pirie had moved too hastily, and they wanted to reopen the negotiations. And so once again, all parties returned to the same bank offices they had sat in the day before. This time, the room to the left was a bit more crowded. Five partners showed up on behalf of the firm: John T. Pirie, Sam C. Pirie, Robert Scott, George Scott and Andrew MacLeish. The debate was spirited and prolonged. Shedd later observed, "The partners debated the matter with me for two hours...finally it being evident that it was the only opportunity for Carson Pirie Scott & Company to continue retail business on State Street...[they offered] Mr. Selfridge a bonus of $150,000 which Mr. Selfridge instructed me to accept."

And finally, everyone was happy. Carson Pirie Scott had secured a home on State Street in an exquisite building, which it would ultimately occupy for more than one hundred years. Shedd was a hero of sorts, garnering profuse thanks from all parties in the transaction. And "mile-a-minute Harry" had walked away from the whirlwind months of legal contracts with a hefty bonus in his pocket. In fact, he was quite proud of himself. For the rest of his life, he boasted, "I am the only man ever to buy a business from five Jews and sell it to seven Scotchmen at a profit."

After the sale, Selfridge dropped out of sight for several years. He would emerge from the shadows once again in 1909, when he opened up a department store on Oxford Street in London, running it in the style and tradition he had learned from his days at Marshall Field and Company. Today, Selfridges & Company is one of the United Kingdom's largest department store chains and a remarkable tourist draw. Not bad for a brash young man from the woods of Wisconsin.

Chapter 5

THE GOLDEN YEARS ON STATE

The city is so unbelievably beautiful. It's one of the greatest cities on the planet. My heart beats differently when I'm in Chicago. It slows down and I feel more at ease.
—*Jeremy Piven, American actor and film producer*

As soon as Carson Pirie Scott and Company settled into its new home at the corner of State and Madison, it quickly expanded farther south on State, adding a new five-bay extension drafted by architect Daniel H. Burnham. Although Burnham did not copy Sullivan's exquisite ornamentation in exact detail, he created a similar design that blended seamlessly with the existing store. Later, in 1927, Burnham's sons erected a fifteen-story structure at the northwest corner of Wabash and Monroe, which would serve as Carson's Men's Store. In 1950, the busy Scots absorbed yet another building, a ten-story structure on Monroe that had been built in 1940 by architect Louis Kroman. And finally, in 1960, one last addition designed by architects Holabird and Root extended the store south on State once again. The end result was a retail palace with approximately 974,000 square feet of floor space and an exterior that majestically dominated the city's busiest intersection.

Of course, the building's interior was just as superb as the stunning façade. Upon entering the rounded double vestibule, a shopper would immediately be awed by the gleaming mahogany ceiling and walls, mosaic marble floor and decorative bronze-colored ironwork that covered the radiator grills. The dramatic twin columns that flanked the interior entryway like sentries

After several acquisitions, the original building extended far down State Street.

were crowned with detailed sculptural plaster and finished with a patina that evoked memories of aged bronze. Looking back toward the street, one might notice sunlight shimmering in intricate patterns through the ornate scrollwork arching over the glass-topped doorways. And after dark, an elaborate bronzed pendant arc light suspended overhead cast a bright glow through its milky white glass globe and beckoned customers to enter.

Once inside the store, the vast panorama of the first floor was broken only by the slender white pillars that marched through the space, their decorative capitals drawing the eye upward and accentuating the open, airy feel. This was quite a departure from the labyrinth of small, dark rooms that characterized most of the older buildings, which depended on interior support walls as load-bearing mechanisms. Rows of mahogany and glass showcases displayed the fine merchandise astride a wide main aisle paved with pale Tennessee pink marble and edged with contrasting gray-green polished stone. On the east side of the store, a delicate metal grillwork screened a wide staircase with elaborately embellished balustrades and a bank of eight modern elevators. The elevators themselves were a work of art; each cab was topped by an iron-scrolled skylight that allowed natural light to trickle in through the glassed shaft.

In fact, the whole building was designed to admit the maximum amount of natural light. Electric lighting remained somewhat of a novelty at the time, although Sullivan's masterpiece did have a full complement of incandescent and arc fixtures. Regardless, the soft glow of sunlight cast a feeling of warmth that no harsh electric bulb could duplicate. To further enhance this effect, the architects placed a band of Luxfer prismatic glass along the top of each massive plate-glass display window on the first and second floors, which captured and cast light into the far recesses of the room. As a result, the store exuded a brightness and comfort rarely matched in that era.

The first floor on State carried an immense array of accessories for any stylish lady. The latest in millinery fashions from Paris, gloves, jewelry, handbags and parasols adorned each showcase. An advertisement of the day extolled the qualities of Onyx hosiery: "Pure Thread Dyed Silk... Best Made in America...every possible shade or color to match any shoe or gown." The hosiery was scandalously pricy at $2.25 per pair, but every pair was "guaranteed," and the color selection—which included fanciful shades such as wisteria, Copenhagen blue, American beauty, amethyst and natural pongee—was sure to delight even the most discriminating shopper. Helpful sales clerks stood at the ready to present the large selection of exotic perfumes from France, England and Spain. Of course, the store also carried the newest innovations in ladies' toilet articles, such as the E.C. Webster and Sons quadruple silver-plated hair curling set, the earliest predecessor of today's heated curling irons.

The Wabash extension's first few floors catered mostly to men, and that lobby floor displayed a fine assortment of luggage, leather goods, coins, stamps and men's furnishings. There were cameras and books and even an optician who could fashion a new pair of spectacles for those who had difficulty reading the small print in the leather-bound volumes. After sorting through all the treasures on the first floor, a shopper could choose to ascend

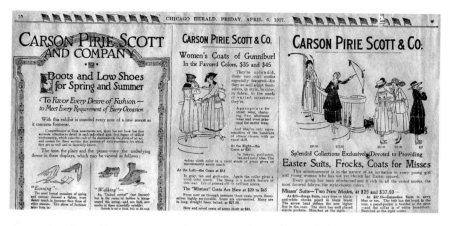

Carson's always advertised for the fashion-conscious shopper.

Carson's carried a wide array of the latest bestselling books.

to the upper floors for clothing and home goods or take a quick ride on the elevator to Carson's budget store. The "bargain basement" concept was a relatively new feature of downtown department stores. Gordon Selfridge had created one on the lower level during his time at the Marshall Field store—reportedly to the great chagrin of Mr. Field himself—but it had turned out to be a grand success and quickly won Field's blessing. Soon, Carson's and other stores followed suit. The idea made a lot of sense; it allowed retailers an opportunity to sell through slow-moving or discontinued merchandise, and it provided a great value for frugal patrons. It also enticed a whole new demographic of shoppers into the store: those whose finances usually restricted them to more bargain-minded retailers such as The Fair or the Beehive. Once inside, the person would perhaps be seduced into buying a few high-end trinkets and might be more likely to return for special-occasion gifts when funds permitted.

In later years, the lower level included the Tartan Tray Cafeteria, a quick and budget-friendly alternative to the more elegant full-service restaurants in the building. In fact, in-store food service was likely another innovation that could be traced back to Harry Selfridge. During his reign at Field's, he had been the one who convinced Field of the merits of such a plan. At that time, dining options for unescorted women were limited. Although men could get a hearty hot lunch at any number of dark and rowdy saloons, a proper lady would never set foot into such an establishment. Female shoppers would have to return home for a midday meal or grow hungry and faint if their shopping day was extended. To avoid this—and to keep the ladies (and their wallets) in the store for a longer period—Carson's provided a charming restaurant called the Tea Room on the eighth floor. Here, female patrons could rest and enjoy a delightful beverage along with a light lunch of salad or fancy pastries. Tea cost fifteen cents per pot and came in eight varieties, including the familiar English Breakfast tea and the exotic-sounding basket-fired uncolored Japan tea. For those who preferred a bolder refreshment, champagne ginger ale sold for twenty cents per glass.

Lunch was quite a bargain as well. For a light snack, a generous slice of French coffee cake could be had for fifteen cents, while a more filling meal of crab or chicken salad sold for seventy-five cents. Splurging on the fresh lobster salad at ninety cents would set a diner back more than a dollar by the time a beverage and tip were added to the check. And if there was still room for dessert, Carson's offered nearly thirty ice cream choices, including vanilla with kumquat sauce, and the delectable-sounding "Special caramel ice cream cake" that was an indulgence at thirty cents.

Of course, with Carson's in-store dining, male customers didn't need to leave the store to seek sustenance either; the mahogany-paneled Men's Grill on the eighth floor served up a varied menu of steaks, chops and other substantial fare. The room smelled of finely aged leather, expensive cigars and polished wood. Imposing columns of gleaming red African onyx added to the masculine yet sophisticated style. After eating, a gentleman could relax in one of the generously upholstered red leather captain's chairs and enjoy a leisurely smoke while chatting with his pals. There was also a bank of modern telephones for the businessman who chose to conduct transactions in an atmosphere of quiet elegance. The grill had its own private elevator, and women were strictly prohibited every day except Saturday, when they would be admitted if—and only if—they were accompanied by their husbands. One fine afternoon, two women, perhaps emboldened by all the recent talk of suffrage, ventured into the forbidden territory without a male escort. They explained their behavior by stating that the Men's Grill offered "fast service, good food, and cheaper prices than a comparable [women's] restaurant." The male patrons were aghast, and one asked the hostess, "Why don't you throw them out?" They were ultimately served, but not before the waiter asked, "Don't you know that men come here to get away from you?"

In those days, shopping at one of the classier city department stores was intended to be a relaxing and pampering experience. Most of the goods were displayed in showcases and behind counters, where attentive and courteous sales associates waited to assist. Patrons could take a seat on comfortable stools that lined the fronts of the counters or on one of the many upholstered chairs that dotted most departments. The articles they desired to inspect would be carried to them and usually presented with a flourish, along with a practiced narrative about the items' features. If shopping became too tiresome, the better stores, such as Field's and Carson's, offered attractive ladies' rest areas that included lavatories, lounge rooms and writing rooms. Carson's had two such suites, one on the third floor and one on the ninth. The rooms were bright and airy, with white columns capped by elaborate silvery capitals. Tufted chaise lounges and fresh greenery decorated the area, and the carved mahogany fretwork screens that hung at the perimeter provided a measure of privacy as well as beauty. And, if a customer felt ill, the store provided an emergency medical room staffed with trained nurses.

The writing rooms offered large comfortable desks equipped with stationery and postcards that allowed patrons to pen a letter to friends or family, detailing their delightful day of shopping or seeing the sights. For tourists, it was perhaps a mark of pride to post a letter back home on the fine linen writing paper embossed with the initials "CPS" at the top. It bespoke of class and refinement, unlike the common penny postcards of the day. Of course, the store also had an extensive stationery department featuring the finest writing implements, notecards, bound leather journals and an array of custom-order products that could be monogrammed or embossed with

Bruce MacLeish (seen here) succeeded his father, Andrew, when the latter retired.

initials, names or addresses. Inexpensive trinkets such as decorative pencil boxes and sealing wax were available and made lovely gifts.

In fact, there were precious few consumer goods and services that were *not* available in the store. There were opticians and jewelers, furriers and tailors, carpeting and furniture, fabrics and linens, toys, household goods, hardware, appliances and sporting goods, a photography shop and even a pet shop. You could get a watch or clock repaired, have your purchases festively wrapped or have a portrait taken and carefully framed. Carson's printed and distributed free train schedules, maps and tourist guides and participated in numerous civic causes. In 1953, it became the first department store chain to sell insurance policies to its customers. During war years, the company held blood drives and used its display windows to promote war bond purchases and voice support for the troops. In many ways, the massive establishment functioned as a small city within a city. In 1935, the State Street store added air conditioning and escalators for the customers' comfort. What a lovely way to spend a hot summer afternoon, reveling in the refreshing coolness while admiring the vast array of goods and services!

But for those who couldn't come to witness the grandeur in person, the store would come to them through mail-order catalogues and a fleet of delivery trucks. Carson's billed itself as "the quickest mail order house in the world." Each season, it published a hefty catalogue called *The Shopper's Economist*. One spring issue was described as "the most complete Shopping Guide ever published—144 pages devoted to good form in woman's wear, the correct Spring Styles as shown in our seventy departments being accurately described and handsomely illustrated."

Carson Pirie Scott also followed the early example set by Potter Palmer, and later by Marshall Field, in its generous return policy. One of its ads boldly stated, "Your money back if not satisfied with your purchase—don't have to tell us the reason why—it's enough for us to know you want to trade back." Another advertisement for boys' school suits said, "If you're not quite sure that they're worth $7.00—SEND THEM BACK, at OUR expense— please." Interestingly, the suits sold for only $4.95, so presumably the store was guaranteeing that a buyer would get well more than his money's worth in the deal. A similar ad for ladies' English coaching capes included the tag line, "It pays to do your shopping by mail." The capes, which sold for $6.75, were advertised as "garments [that] are in every respect the equal of others retailed at ten dollars."

This focus on customer satisfaction carried through every facet of the business. Employees were carefully trained and constantly drilled on

Your Souvenir
GUIDE MAP
A Century *of* Progress

★

Self-Escorted Tours

to the

Century *of* Progress Exposition

★

Tours Planned
to fill interestingly and to the
best advantage the time
you have available

Self-Escorted Tour Bureau
is located on the first floor,
State Street side

"UNDER THE CLOCK"

The famous corner entrance of CARSON PIRIE SCOTT & CO., situated on what is said to be the world's busiest corner, at State and Madison Streets. Chicagoans have long made this store a convenient meeting place. Just within these doors is a large and spacious lobby entrance leading directly into the first floor sections of the store, and to the Aisle of States. There are two other entrances on State Street, as well as those on Madison, Wabash and Monroe Street.

★

CARSON PIRIE SCOTT & CO

State Madison
Wabash Monroe

Chicago

The Century of Progress Fair provided an opportunity for merchants to display the latest technology. Carson's added air conditioning and escalators for the fair.

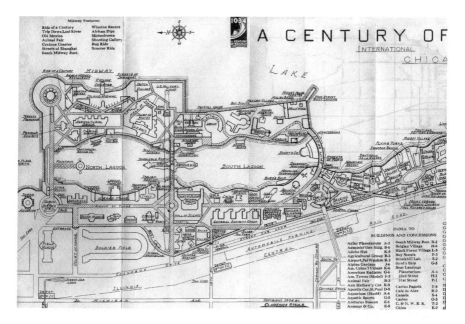

Carson's distributed maps to the tens of thousands of tourists who visited the Century of Progress Fair. Of course, all roads eventually led to State Street.

the importance of respect and proper attitude. An early personnel book reminded workers that "the real boss is our customer." Appearance also mattered; a strictly enforced dress code dictated that female clerks would wear a black skirt and white long-sleeved blouse, neutral hose and a tasteful minimum of makeup and jewelry. Men wore black trousers and a white shirt with a tie. They were also expected to be clean shaven and well groomed. Employees were strongly encouraged to be friendly but were prohibited from crossing the line into a careless or casual demeanor. They could not use any of the amenities designed for guests, such as lounges or writing rooms. Any infractions would result in immediate dismissal. Their job required them to be discreet, courteous, helpful and ever present, anticipating and hopefully surpassing the customers' expectations. For all this, a typical employee in the late 1930s earned about fifteen dollars for six days' work.

Of course, not too many workers complained. Although they were held to high standards, they were in turn treated with respect and professionalism. In spite of its tremendous growth, Carson's continued to operate like the close family-owned business it had started out as. The company's handbook proudly stated, "The personnel policies of Carson Pirie Scott and Company are based on respect for human dignity, and on

Carson's held regular award ceremonies for longtime employees, such as these folks who achieved fifty years with the store.

our recognition of the importance of every individual's contribution to our company." Nor were past employees forgotten; every year the firm held a large Christmas party complete with generous gifts for its retirees so that they could continue to feel part of the company. Workers also received birthday cards and acknowledgement of other major life events. Indeed, both Carson's and Marshall Field's enjoyed a level of employee stability and loyalty rarely seen in other retail businesses. Fifty-year employees were not uncommon, and their work anniversaries never passed without celebration and recognition.

In addition, the company carried its policy of respect into all aspects of its corporate dealings. Carson's was held in high esteem by its competitors and had a sterling reputation of honesty and integrity. For example, managers were strictly forbidden to hire workers from competing stores unless the person's current employer provided confirmation that they were aware of and approved the employee's desire to switch firms. Although the company often boasted in advertisements that its products were superior to or cheaper than offerings from "other retailers," its ads never named a competitor or made a direct comparison. When Marshall Field died, Carson's participated in a full-page tribute to the fallen merchant, and the store—along with many other businesses on State Street—closed its doors on the day of his funeral as a show of respect. All these actions were part of a company philosophy designed to "maintain sound business relations." As the company has long since passed 150 years in business, it's quite obvious that philosophy has proven to be successful.

Chapter 6

CHRISTMAS AT CARSON'S

Now, the essence, the very spirit of Christmas is that we first make believe a thing
is so, and lo, it presently turns out to be so.
—Stephen Leacock, Canadian writer and humorist

The holiday season is a magical time to be a child, and to generations of children, perhaps no place embodied this more than Chicago's State Street. It was a place to believe in the unbelievable, to bask in the enchantment and, for a little while at least, to know that almost anything was possible if you just wished hard enough.

Like all proper magic, most of the wizardry went on behind the scenes, beyond that thin veil between what the eye sees and what the heart knows is true. In fact, just about the time that the final tree ornament was packed away in tissue paper and the last cookie reduced to a pile of crumbs and happy memories, the wizards would already be conjuring up images to dazzle and delight in the next yuletide season.

For most State Street merchants, Christmas began in February. That's when they'd review their results from the past season and the design teams would meet to toss around ideas on how to outdo themselves in the coming year. Once they selected a theme, they would begin to sketch out storyboards to tell the tale throughout the display windows and the store. And that's when the magic would truly begin. While Chicagoans sweltered under hot sunny summer skies, the carpenters and artists would be hard at work crafting the snowmen, Santas, reindeers and elves that would spring to life as winter

No holiday trip to Carson's was complete without a visit with Santa Claus.

approached. The work was difficult and detailed. After all, a child's vision of Santa's sleigh shouldn't be compromised by visible wires, staples or any other manner of shoddy work.

Late spring and early summer were the busiest times for the buyers as well, especially the toy buyers. They needed to anticipate the next coveted doll or decide if little boys would prefer baseball gloves or perhaps footballs next year. Buyers from the largest stores traveled the world to seek out the newest and the most exciting toys to hide under the tree on Christmas morning. Of course, those were simpler times, quaint by comparison to today's world.

Holiday cards and ads heightened the anticipation of a visit from Santa.

Toys were typically made of wood, fabric or tin, not LEDs or motherboards. "Gender stereotyping" was the norm, although no one had ever heard of or used the term. Santa brought little girls fancy baby dolls that cried and wet, miniature tea sets and toy appliances that allowed them to pretend to bake just like mom. There were even toy irons and vacuum cleaners for the aspiring housewife with a cleaning bent. Little boys, on the other hand, received "manly" toys such as sports equipment, toy trucks, tin soldiers, child-sized tool chests or perhaps a chemistry set for the unusually bright and inquiring youngster. Oh sure, the occasional "tomboy" female might get away with asking for a baseball mitt or riding car, but a little boy who requested, for example, a baby doll would be ignored at best, perhaps even dragged to a counselor in an effort to "straighten him out."

In any case, no matter what a child's heart desired, it could be found on State Street. There were more than a dozen major department stores along the avenue, along with assorted other businesses that heralded the beginning of the season with elaborate displays. And in 1934, December in Chicago became even more spectacular with the introduction of the first Christmas Parade. At the time, much of the country was still reeling from the effects of the 1929 stock market crash. Although the economy was improving, shoppers remained reluctant to spend, and the previous Christmas had been a rather dismal time for merchants. Walter Gregory, president of Chicago's State Street Council, dreamt up the idea of a huge parade to welcome Santa—and hopefully more shoppers—to the downtown retail district. Mayor Edward Kelly agreed with the plan, and the inaugural event was scheduled for December 7, 1934.

The day dawned cloudy and miserably cold. Temperatures dipped to fourteen degrees below zero, and the winds howling from the lake quickly turned State Street into a frozen wasteland. The weather wasn't fit for man or beast, but the tenacious Chicago spirit wasn't daunted by a bit of old man winter's wrath. As the appointed time drew near, the crowds began to materialize. Gregory gamely directed the caravan, which included Santa and his helpers, who passed out candy and goodies to people along the route. Soon, the entire street was lined with enthusiastic celebrants. Parents lifted their heavily bundled children onto their shoulders so that the little ones could see, although most were too numbed by the cold to do much more than stare in awe. After the parade ended, families sought refuge in the warm and inviting stores and began to spend at a rate not seen since before the Great Depression. From that day forward, the annual State Street Christmas Parade has been a fixture every holiday season.

Seventeen Ways TO A YOUNG GIRL'S HEART AT CHRISTMASTIME

1. Little suede "little Johns". Green, black, beige, grey, red, brown. Sizes 4 to 9. 4.00.
2. Wool plaid stocking cap. 5.50.
3. Wool skating cap appliqued in a medley of colors. 5.00.
4. Dark brown leather handbag. 4.95.*
5. Handmade knit wool mittens. White, green, red. Small, medium, large. 3.95.
6. Make-up box of quilted pink rayon satin. Contains ten tricks for young beauty. 8.75.*
7. Drawstring carry-all of navy rayon taffeta lined with cerise. Contains six young beauty essentials. Serves as an evening bag, too. 7.50.*
8. Brown shoulder-strap bag, leatherette lined. 4.95.*

9. 10K gold link charm bracelet. 8.00.*
10. 10K gold charms. 1.00 to 5.00 each.*
11. Sterling silver chain bracelet. 1.00.*
12. Sterling silver charms. 75c each.*
13. Charm stick-pins, set of four. 1.00 set.*
   Shown in the photograph above:
14. Wool knit stocking cap. White, green, brown, red, navy. 5.00.
15. White fur mittens with red capeskin palms. Small, medium, large. 4.95.*
16. Swissies all-wool sweater. Red-white, green-red, navy-white. Various patterns. Sizes 10 to 16. 8.95.
17. Full-pleated skirt of imported wool. Red, navy, green, brown. Sizes 10 to 16. 8.95.

*plus excise tax

■ GIRLS' SHOP, FIFTH FLOOR   ■ SHOES, THIRD FLOOR   ■ GIRLS' HATS, FIFTH FLOOR

A gift from Carson's was sure to be a hit.

Encouraged by the response, the merchants began to create elaborate themed windows to draw attention to their businesses. Some stores developed characters to tell their stories, and these sometimes spun off to independent fame. The iconic Rudolph the Red-Nosed Reindeer was a Christmas character developed for retailer Montgomery Ward. He came very close to being named Rollo Reindeer or Reginald Reindeer until his creator, Robert May, finally decided on Rudolph. Down the street, Wieboldt's had Cinnamon Bear, a perpetually cheerful little stuffed bear that ended up with his own television show. He encouraged children to come see him—and all his shiny toys—as often as possible. Marshall Field and Company, never to be outdone, created an entire cast of characters led by Uncle Mistletoe, a jolly, impish, winged little man who could fly like a bee and helped out Santa by identifying all the good and kind children in the world. Uncle Mistletoe lived in the Cozy Cloud Cottage at Field's, along with Aunt Holly; Freddie Field Mouse and his family; Tony Pony; Otto the Elephant; elves Olio, Molio and Rolio; Aunt Judy; Skippy Monkey; Michael O'Hare; and Obediah Pig. Uncle Mistletoe and his friends also spawned a television show, along with numerous records and a Golden Book.

Carson's dabbled in proprietary characters, but they never gained traction in the manner of the others. After a few nondescript teddy bears, the company introduced Martian Bear in the late 1970s. Martian Bear was a large costumed character that greeted children at the State Street store. Quite honestly, the character resembled a lanky large-eared mouse more than a bear, and his silver vest and upside-down funnel hat didn't seem to have much of an association with Christmas, but he was amusing, if perhaps a little bizarre. Later, the store created a private label line of plush toys called Furbles. Furbles were brightly colored shaggy monsters with names like Raz, Walter and Mot. Again, these toys didn't evoke memories of Christmases past, but they were a hit with the kids. Unfortunately, they received a lukewarm reception from parents and were subsequently discontinued.

Where Carson's really shone was in its window displays. Like Field's, Carson's did not usually display merchandise in the main Christmas windows. They were created as a sort of gift to the city, telling stories to amuse and enchant passersby. Of course, the ultimate goal was to draw shoppers into the store, and in that they were very successful. Although Field's windows were quite popular, sometimes the crowds that came to view them were so dense that children would see little more than a sea of adult legs in front of them. Carson's, however, had a special advantage: its breathtaking domed entrance. Workers would place characters on top of

Sparkling lights and glitter adorned the store and welcomed shoppers.

the rotunda that tied to the window theme. For example, when they told the story of *The Nutcracker*, a towering nutcracker figurine stood at attention above the door, alerting shoppers from blocks away about what lay in store for them when they arrived at the fabulous windows. For *A Christmas Carol*, a larger-than-life Bob Cratchit smiled joyfully down on the crowds below, with Tiny Tim perched on his shoulders. A banner above proclaimed "God bless us, everyone!" And for *Amahl and the Night Visitors*, a solemn and holy Nativity scene brought a hush to the noisy crowds that gathered.

For a child, the bustle, noise and twinkling lights on State could feel a bit overwhelming, but suddenly a vision would appear in the distance. The whole family might speculate on what it heralded as they hurried through a gentle snowfall. Soon it would come into focus. Was it a giant nutcracker? Or perhaps a family of forest animals preparing for Christmas night? Perhaps it was just a massive tree, its lights and ornaments glittering in the reflected glow of streetlamps. And then it was time to follow the story in the windows, marveling at the animated figures that danced and twirled as if they'd come to life. One year, a continuous façade of make-believe storefronts framed each window on State, making it appear to visitors that they had suddenly been transported to a quaint village in a far-off land.

The Christmas Villages façade transported visitors to faraway lands.

Festive garlands decorated the Monroe Street entrance.

Eventually, the cold and the wind became unbearable, and it was time to pass through the elaborate entrance and into the store. It would take a minute for a person's eyes to adjust to the sudden brightness, and those wearing eyeglasses had to remove them to wipe away the sudden fog created by the abrupt temperature change. Children would stamp their feet to shake off the snow and perhaps to bring a bit of circulation back to their frozen toes. The main aisle was always decorated in splendor. Strands of garland or crystal snaked from the ceiling across the light fixtures, and brightly colored ornaments were everywhere. There were twinkling lights and sprigs of evergreen and banners that counted down the days to Christmas. The elegant store seemed to have been transformed into a holiday castle!

Of course, kids always wanted to head straight to the toy department on the fifth floor, but mom might want to stop first at the Christmas Aisle of Gifts on the second floor. It was the perfect place to pick up impressive yet inexpensive trinkets for friends or neighbors. After growing exasperated by the children's whining and begging, the family would finally ascend to the fifth floor. Perhaps dad would shepherd the youngsters toward the toy department while mom browsed the Yuletide Shop for ornaments, wrapping paper and bows. Carson's carried just about any decoration one could imagine. There were lights and tree skirts and stocking stuffers and Nativity scenes. By the time dad returned with the kids in tow, mom's arms were usually filled with packages.

Now it was time for the highlight of the entire trip: a visit with Santa! During the Christmas season, Santa camped out in the eighth-floor auditorium atop a small stage. The jolly old soul perched on a massive wooden throne with exquisitely carved detail. His beard was as white as snow, and his girth seemed likely to collapse the throne into splinters. A band of helpers dressed in elf costumes kept the children moving along smoothly in line. In spite of the anticipation leading up to the moment, and the lengthy mental list the child had prepared from the trip to the toy department, many were struck dumb or suddenly terrified by the face-to-face meeting. Slightly older children could sometimes soldier through with only the slightest trace of a grimace on their frozen faces, but the littlest ones often howled like banshees. Santa would do his best to remain cheerful, shouting, "Ho Ho Ho!" as an assistant snapped a black-and-white photo of the encounter. For a small price, mom and dad could purchase the print, framed in cardboard, to record that year's Christmas, when the children were still young enough to believe that reindeers could fly.

The story of the Nutcracker delighted children and adults alike.

The Nutcracker banners announced that year's window theme.

And then, blinded by the camera's flash, the disoriented child would be hustled off stage by the elves, who would press a small coloring book or mesh stocking of candy into the youngster's hand before handing him or her off to mom and dad. Upon leaving the auditorium, the family would pass through a long corridor that was lined with silver-framed pictures of all the celebrities who had visited Carson's. There were actors and actresses, politicians and royalty and people who were famous enough to make the hallway cut but not quite famous enough to recognize or remember. One more trip down the elevator, and finally it was time to bundle back up for the long, cold trudge back to the bus stop or family car.

The kids would be exhausted and sometimes needed to be carried on dad's shoulder. But that night, when they settled into their beds, they would dream about what they had seen and would hold on to that memory for years to come. Years later, perhaps when they had children of their own, they might have stumbled across the faded and bent cardboard-backed photo and—for just a brief moment—remembered what it felt like when life was simpler and magic just meant that one had to believe.

Chapter 7
WORLD WAR II AND BEYOND

Always remember that the future comes one day at a time.
—*Dean Acheson, American statesman*

As the war in Europe raged, the U.S. economy was in turmoil. The war effort greatly increased the need for production, and unemployment soon became virtually nonexistent. Women, students, retirees and all other able-bodied citizens streamed into the workforce to support our forces abroad. At the war's peak, about 40 percent of all domestic production was channeled overseas, and numerous commodities required strict rationing. Many foods—including meat, cheese, coffee, sugar, butter, dried fruit and canned goods—were available only with government-issued ration coupons. The same applied to necessities such as clothing, gasoline and fuel oil. In addition, all manufacturing of non-critical goods like new cars and appliances was temporarily halted to divert the raw goods into the production of war machinery.

The idea of rationing was designed to ensure that the limited goods available would be spread equally across the population and to prevent hoarding. The very poor would have the same access to food and clothing as the very rich. Personal incomes were at an all-time high due to the availability of jobs, and the demand for increased production spawned long work days and abundant overtime pay. Unfortunately, there was precious little for the consumer to actually buy, and uncertainty about the future caused most people to stash away the money in fear. Of course, this sudden increase in

The 1965 World Import Fair showcased goods from around the world.

manufacturing and wealth came with a downside; without price controls, the nation risked out-of-control inflation. Therefore, in August 1941, the Office of Price Administration (OPA) was established to impose limits for consumer goods prices and rents. Many stores even posted these "ceiling lists" to assure customers that their prices conformed to OPA rules.

During these years, Carson Pirie Scott maintained a solid retail clientele, but in general, Chicago's wholesale market was bleeding red ink. By 1942, the partners were forced to make the difficult decision to shut down the wholesale business, which was becoming a drain on the entire enterprise. The only exception was the highly profitable floor coverings division. Carson's retained that segment and moved it to a new home in the massive Merchandise Mart, which was at that time still owned by competitor Marshall Field and Company. By 1945, the painful liquidation was finished, and the company had come full circle to its original inception as a retail-only establishment. But the enterprising Scots had no intention of becoming stagnant; expansion and growth still remained squarely in their line of vision.

As soon as the war overseas wound down, Carson's found itself fighting a small-scale war of its very own. In the summer of 1945, New York retailer R.H. Macy & Company made a bid to swallow up the store. For a while, it looked as though it would succeed. Newspapers and financial analysts buzzed about the New York invasion. In the end, however, all the remaining family

Mrs. Smith

CONSULTS HER DECORATOR

You guessed it . . . our fictitious Mrs. Smith *is her own decorator* . . . just as you can be with Wishmaker, Carson's magic means to achieve charm and decorative distinction in your home.

Wishmaker simply sets the pace for you with three home-furnishing themes—Traditional, Modern, and, soon, American Provincial. In each group specially designed wallpapers, fabrics, floor coverings, and superb furniture are perfectly coordinated in period . . . but you've leeway galore in your color and pattern selection.

You're really on your own with Carson's Wishmaker . . . to pick, and choose, and assemble to your heart's content . . . to weave your own personal expression into *your* home . . . guided, unerringly, by Wishmaker, but decorated by *you.*

And it's all so sure, so simple . . . for everything is right here, and everything here is right . . . in the Wishmaker Shop at Carson's.

Wishmaker Shop, ninth floor

The Wishmaker Shop was an in-store interior design center.

members from the Pirie, Scott and MacLeish clans voted their shares of stock in a unified block and were able to fend off the corporate marauders. But now, the families realized that they would need more capital to grow the company. The Louis Sullivan building they occupied was approaching forty years of age and would soon require about $3 million in repairs. The iron anchors that held in place the massive terra-cotta cornice that crowned the store were failing. Removal and repair would be prohibitively expensive, so the cornice was permanently removed, and a few other modifications were made to the building in a 1948 renovation. To infuse some cash, the partners decided it was time to take the company public. In early 1946, Carson Pirie Scott and Company issued fifty thousand shares of preferred stock. It also established a pension and profit-sharing plan for employees. For the first time in its nearly one-hundred-year history, the immense store was no longer a family-owned business.

By the 1950s, the company was relatively flush with cash and ready to expand. The postwar era had heralded a massive migration from the city to the suburbs, and retailers were following closely behind. Carson's opened its first suburban location in Evergreen Park Plaza, which was one of America's earliest major regional malls when it was built in 1952. The 293,000-square-foot store remains in operation as of this writing, although the mall surrounding it shut down in May 2013. Next the company opened a much smaller location of only 110,000 square feet at Woodmar Mall in Hammond, Indiana. In 1956, Carson's added two more stores to its growing roster: Edens Plaza in Wilmette, Illinois (212,000 square feet), and Hillside Shopping Center in Hillside, Illinois (125,000 square feet). Over the next two decades, Carson Pirie Scott would continue to expand rapidly throughout the Chicago and Peoria markets, with stores ranging from the very large (Lakehurst Mall in Waukegan, Illinois, at 231,000 square feet) to the rather diminutive (Gateway at Riverside Plaza in Chicago, a scant 11,000-square-foot city store).

While the suburban development was flourishing, there was also plenty of change afoot on State Street. In 1958, C. Virgil Martin was named president and chief executive officer of Carson Pirie Scott and Company after John T. Pirie Jr. retired. It was the first time in the company's long history that it would be led by someone not related to one of the founders. Mr. Martin was a bold leader and not afraid to take chances, and he forged ahead with an aggressive expansion plan. He believed in the power of diversity, both in business and in society. He has been credited with being the first of the major State Street retailers to knock down the "color barrier" by hiring African

Shop at home . . . write Carson Pirie Scott & Co.,
Add 15c postage per item outside delivery area.

**Perpetual classic . . .
to be bowed, beaued!**

Town & Country's dashing
fashion: the wing collar . . .
artist bowed; the dramatic
buttons . . . pocket accented.
Burlington's pin point rayon
in grey, brown, 10-20. **14.95**
College Almanac Fashions,
Fourth Floor

52

**Give your feet a treat:
bubble-soled booties**

Angel Treads with foam
rubber innersole to keep
you literally walking on
air! Instep elasticized—
in washable cherry,
blue, green or plaid
corduroy. S-M-L. Pr.,
1.98.

55   College Notions,
First Floor

**Good news . . .
the garter brief**

Lux-ees by Luxite . . . the
pantie that banishes
bothersome girdles,
garter belts! Non-run
nylon in white, pink,
blue, black, 24 to 30
waists. **2.50**

56   College Lingerie,
Third Floor

Almanac · 1951

**Clear sailing . . . the
slim skirt, tailored blouse**

College Town's pure wool
flannel peg-top skirt . . .
in menswear grey, brown;
wine, navy, dark green,
purple, 9-17. **7.95.**
Classic of Boston's
convertible collar shirt
in white, gold, pink,
green or bittersweet
broadcloth, 9-15. **5.95**

College Almanac Fashions
Fourth Floor

53

54

**Hand Dryer . . . for
hair, nails, lingerie**

Handy Hannah Deluxe
never keeps you waiting!
Light weight, chrome
finish, temp-controlled,
. . . with removable,
adjusto-base and guar-
antee, **9.95.** Also, blue
enamel, **6.95.**

57   College Helpers,
Seventh Floor

**Middle magic: your
contour belt**

Victory's saddle leather
success . . . a sure fire
cinch to whittle your
middle, make the most
of separates. Black,
brown, navy, red, kelly,
turf and natural. Sizes
24 to 34.   **3.50**

58   College Belts,
First Floor

Carson Pirie Scott & Co.

Ads in fashion magazines such as this one in *Mademoiselle* appealed to the college student of
the 1950s.

mademoiselle for august 1951

Carson's College Almanac

Leaves and eyes are turning . . . to the autumn array of your light, bright, right corduroy mix-match co-ordinates

By Korday Sportswear . . . to give you the key to an all-around wardrobe! Lots of change for little change . . . a fourfold story of fashion, fit, fabric and fun to relate or separate at your whim.

Boy jacket in red and green tartan, **19.95.** Skirt, **7.95**; solid jacket, **16.95** — in dark green, russet, red, gold, purple, 10-18. Cap to match, **2.50**

Corduroy Skirt and spun knit nylon blouse in russet, gold, purple, cyclamen, dark green and black, 10-18. Each **10.95**

Corduroy slacks in dark green, black, brown, grey, **8.95.** Also, pedal pushers to match, **7.95.** V-front vest in dark green, russet, gold, purple, black, red, **5.95.** Tartan broadcloth shirt in navy, or red, with green, **5.95.** All in sizes 10 to 18.

Send your orders to Carson Pirie Scott & Co., Chicago. Add 15c postage per item outside delivery area.

Carson Pirie Scott&Co.

College wardrobes have changed considerably over the past sixty years.

Carson's introduces its new IBM computer credit system.

Frederick Scott throws a switch to activate Carson's new closed-circuit television system.

VIRGIL MARTIN

C. Virgil Martin revitalized the store with his strong leadership and aggressive marketing.

Americans to work at the store. In a move almost as radical for the era, he also promoted women to upper management positions. Martin strongly believed in equal opportunity and championed the cause well before it was politically correct or mandated by law. He was a proponent of minority housing initiatives, and in 1967, he was elected president of the Leadership Council for Metropolitan Open Communities, a Chicago-based grass-roots organization that worked to develop open housing legislation.

Under Martin's reign, promotional activity at State Street was bolder and more frequent. In 1959, a ramp that served as a models' runway was installed above a bank of counters for daily college fashion shows. His attempt to draw younger customers into the store was successful, and Carson's soon began to cultivate a reputation as a more casual, relaxed and slightly "hipper" venue than Marshall Field's. As Christmas 1959 approached, Martin had a row of brand-new General Electric quartz heat lamps installed in front of the windows on State. Although the original purpose was to make Christmas window shopping more pleasant during the subzero weather, it quickly stirred an idea for an outlandish and eye-catching promotion. On a bitterly cold winter day, Carson's hired a bevy of beautiful young models to show off a new cruise wear collection. The girls posed in swimwear and shorts outside under the lamps, apparently quite comfortable despite the frigid temperatures. The stunt generated a great deal of publicity, with even the jaded daily newspapers sending out staff photographers to capture the scene.

The store appeared to be constantly in motion, modernizing and reinventing itself at every turn. Also in 1959, it closed the Maypool and Georgian Room restaurants on the eighth floor and in their place opened a large and attractive new restaurant called the Heather House. It boasted a large menu and fast, friendly service, but the focal point of the room was the massive panoramic mural of Edinburgh, Scotland, that covered an entire curved wall. It was painted by an artist named A.R. Gordon and evoked the feeling of a gently rolling Scottish landscape. The soft and elegant pastels capture iconic landmarks such as Edinburgh Castle, the Firth of Forth, Holy Rood Palace and a view from the Dean Bridge that spans the steep valley of the Water of Leith. The restaurant was a peaceful oasis in an otherwise hectic city. Carson's later opened Heather House locations in some of the suburban stores, but none matched the beauty of the original.

Unfortunately, on March 29, 1968, disaster struck. A rash of suspicious fires broke out in rapid succession along State Street, involving Carson's, Wieboldt's and Montgomery Ward's. Each of the fires, which all erupted within a one-hour period, began in a stockroom and quickly spread. Wieboldt's employees were able to extinguish the flames at their store before firefighters arrived, and it only sustained minor damage, but Carson's and Ward's weren't as lucky. Ward's experienced significant loss, but Carson's was by far the hardest hit. Fire Commissioner Robert Quinn called it "one of the worst downtown fires I have ever seen." It began when simultaneous blazes burst out in at least three different areas of the store, on the second, sixth and seventh floors. Customers and employees were immediately evacuated as dozens of pieces of fire equipment crowded State Street and struggled to get hoses and ladders to the upper floors and roof. At about the same time, reports were starting to roll in about the blazes at the other two stores.

Although fire department officials hesitated to go on record and call it arson until their investigation was completed, a clerk at Wieboldt's reported that she saw two men toss something over a partition just before she noticed a puff of smoke and fire. In a later interview, John Pirie Jr. estimated his store's losses were in the millions of dollars and said the fires "definitely are arson. We have evidence of arson. Turpentine was found

The iconic Heather House Restaurant featured a massive mural of Edinburgh, Scotland.

Firemen evacuate the State Street store after a series of arson fires erupted.

in five different areas. The fire department has photographic evidence of this." As a precaution, Chicago Police brought in canine corps to patrol the streets and watch for looters or other suspicious activity before the flames were even extinguished. Just a few days later, while the investigation was still in its early stages, a minor fire also occurred at Goldblatt Bros., another State Street retailer. It began in a basement storeroom, but the store's sprinkler system quickly extinguished it. It appeared that a serial arsonist was prowling the corridors of State Street, but no one was ever arrested or charged with the crimes.

The devastating arson fire caused millions of dollars in damages.

A customer peeks in the store to view the damage after the 1968 arson.

Carson's managed to reopen just five days after the fire, but only about 30 percent of the selling areas were operational. The damage was extensive, especially to the seventh floor. Besides the actual destruction from the fire, the building and much of the merchandise sustained water and smoke damage. Some areas of the store were closed for more than six months as they struggled to rebuild. They did eventually rebound from the losses, however, and in 1970, Sullivan's beautiful building at State and Madison Streets was declared an official Chicago landmark and was also listed on the National Register of Historic Places. Unfortunately, the new decade also brought slow growth for the department store sector. The city's population had been experiencing a rather steep decline as more and more people moved to the suburbs, and more competition was moving into the area, including Neiman-Marcus, I. Magnin and Lord & Taylor.

Carson's management had anticipated some of these changes and had already started expanding into other industries, especially food service and hospitality. One of its earliest acquisitions was Honey Bear Farm, a resort that sat just over the Illinois-Wisconsin border on Powers Lake. Its namesake was a cuddly cartoon bear cub whose adventures with Firepot, his donkey friend, were captured in a story book. And although Honey Bear was fictional, Firepot was a real donkey that lived on the farm, and children could visit and sometimes pet the animal. The resort, which dated back to the 1940s, featured a restaurant with a huge fireplace and an equally large bear in the lobby, and it was extremely popular with the hordes of tourists who descended on southern Wisconsin each summer. Its Sunday brunch drew impressive crowds. After Carson's purchased the property in the 1960s, it expanded to include gift shops, a bakery and a sausage factory that supplied its department stores and restaurants. Although the enterprise was extremely successful for many years, the opening of a nearby mega-amusement park in 1976 caused sales to stumble, and in 1985, the complex was closed and the land sold to a developer.

Carson's also branched out into country clubs with the 1969 purchase of Nordic Hills in Itasca, Illinois, which included two ten-story tower hotel buildings adjacent to an eighteen-hole golf course. Following that, in the mid-1970s, the company bought the Indian Lakes Country Club property in nearby Bloomindale with the intent of building a resort. It hired architect Don Erickson, who had once apprenticed with Frank Lloyd Wright. Erickson disdained the typical hotel style, which he characterized as "stark, non-ending and uninteresting corridors and shoebox-like guestrooms." Instead, he created a Caribbean-style haven that included a central atrium filled with

John Pirie Jr. examines the wares of Junior Achievement members that the store sponsored.

Carson's warehouse store allowed the public to shop for special bargains.

THE DAY WE MOVED THE POPULATION OF KALAMAZOO

That slight population explosion at O'Hare International Airport recently was 83,700 people moving from one place to another through the world's busiest airport. Like everyone in Kalamazoo, or Santa Monica, or Pawtucket being airlifted in one day.

Thirty thousand meals and a hundred thousand pieces of luggage later, a few misplaced children restored, and the longest day was over.

Whether you come from Pasadena, Utica or Paris, you're welcome at O'Hare. And, next trip, pause in the Airport for a quick cup of cheer, or dine leisurely on Chef Gallo's breast of chicken Kiev in the Seven Continents. See you soon?

O'HARE AIRPORT RESTAURANTS

Carson *Pirie* *Scott & Co*

Carson's airport restaurants and in-flight catering represented a large percentage of its income before it returned to its department store roots.

lush tropical foliage. The rooms were hexagonal-shaped modules set off a zigzag corridor. Each of the three hundred oversized rooms included a view of the indoor atrium, the beautiful surrounding landscaping or the golf course. It opened for business in 1982 and was sold by Carson's to the First Hospitality Group in 1999.

In 1980, Carson Pirie Scott borrowed $108 million to buy Dobbs Houses, Inc., a food service and restaurant chain that had its beginnings in Depression-era Tennessee. In 1962, the small chain of counter-service-only diners that specialized in breakfasts and home-cooked meals bought out its chief competitor, Toddle House, which ran a chain of more than two hundred similar restaurants. The combined company grew rapidly and soon expanded into airport restaurants, gift shops, newsstands and in-flight catering. By the time Carson's purchased the enterprise, it held the number-two market share in these areas, behind only Marriott Corp. for in-flight catering and Host International for airport shops and restaurants. Chicago's O'Hare Airport, once the nation's busiest, featured two of Carson's restaurants: a full-service restaurant called Seven Continents, which was located on the upper concourse between Terminals 2 and 3, and a Tartan Tray Cafeteria on the main level.

Carson's food service division did quite well for many years. In fact, airline catering and restaurants accounted for more than half of the company's operating earnings by 1982. In spite of this, the company didn't lose sight of its origins as a department store and continued to grow the retail division. Back in 1961, it had acquired the Block & Kuhl Company in Peoria, a chain of twenty department stores across the region. Although that purchase had doubled its number of locations, Carson Pirie Scott and Company still remained just a regional store, with all its locations sited in Illinois and northern Indiana. That would soon change, however, in ways that no one could anticipate.

Chapter 8

WINDS OF CHANGE

To improve is to change; to be perfect is to change often.
—Winston Churchill

In 1983, a new CEO came on board: former Federal Express Corporation president Peter Wilmott. Wilmott desperately wanted to put Carson's on the map, both figuratively and literally. In 1984, he engineered the purchase of the casual clothing giant County Seat. Although the acquisition cost Carson's $71 million, County Seat operated 269 stores scattered over thirty-three states, with annual sales approaching $200 million per year by the early '80s. For the first time, Carson's sales topped $1 billion, and it could now truly consider itself a nationwide retail presence. Later that year, it also acquired MacDonald Companies, a mail-order catalogue and direct-marketing merchandiser.

Although Carson Pirie Scott had always had a friendly rivalry with Marshall Field's, the two stores positioned themselves for slightly different audiences. Field's tended to appeal to the higher-end shopper, or at least those who harbored such aspirations, while Carson's reached out to the middle class. Over the years, however, the gap between the two had widened. Carson's was slowly developing a reputation as a store for the price-conscious shopper, and that's an identity it didn't want. Wilmott appointed the savvy and bold Dennis Bookshester to shake up the retail division. Bookshester immediately began to bring in higher-quality and more fashionable clothing lines to draw in new customers, and he launched an aggressive advertising

A display window filled with purses entices Carson's core customer, the middle-upper-class woman.

campaign. Its slogan "Come to the right place!" seemed to resonate with customers, and sales increased dramatically in response, leaping from about $84 in sales per square foot to $133 in one short year.

Another innovation he introduced was a store-within-a-store concept called the Corporate Level. In many ways, the idea copied Marshall Field's iconic 28 Shop, but instead of appealing to socialites, Carson's new shop was aimed at female executives. It opened two hours earlier and closed two hours later than the rest of the store, and like the 28 Shop, it had a separate entrance attended by a doorman. The elegant boutique was stocked with designer clothing suitable for business wear, expensive shoes and tasteful accessories. It included services such as a dry cleaner, shoe repair and copier service. There was a juice bar and gourmet deli, gift-wrapping and stationery services. For those wanting even more, a small annual fee would provide access to a fashion consultant and personal shopper, plus the use of private meeting rooms as needed. The concept was so successful that it soon rolled out a version for men and considered plans to introduce stand-alone stores in some markets. Soon, Carson's growing reputation as a high-fashion retailer gained even more traction when it was chosen as the bridal wear consultant for Robert Altman's film *A Wedding*, which was shot largely in the Chicago area.

In 1987, Carson Pirie Scott bought Donaldson's, a department store chain with twelve locations in the Minneapolis area. About this time, the company decided that it was time to return to its department store roots and began the slow process of divesting itself of some of its other businesses. The first to go was its Dobbs Houses in-flight catering and airport terminal concessions, which included restaurants and gift shops at more than forty airports. Carson's sold the business for an impressive $390 million to Greyhound Corporation, which had recently sold its bus lines to concentrate on its travel and leisure businesses. The announcement of the deal caused Carson's stocks to soar by more than $11 a share. Wilmott announced that the wholesale floor coverings division and some smaller restaurant groups were also up for sale, although he hoped that they could be sold to their current management and employees rather than an outsider.

Around this time, a company named Baytree Investors Inc. made a bid to buy Carson's. The group, which had purchased Wieboldt's a year earlier, specialized in leveraged buyouts and had a history of questionable practices. It had virtually no retail experience or, for that matter, interest in learning the industry; it was the financial equivalent of a "chop shop." Wilmott dismissed Baytree as "corporate pirates," and Carson's board immediately rejected its $347 million bid. Baytree was persistent, however, and tendered a second offer. Fearing a hostile takeover, the board immediately declared a "poison pill" dividend. The poison pill strategy is a legal maneuver that makes targeted companies less appealing to would-be raiders. In general, it is a change to a business's financial plan that requires an exorbitant dividend to be paid to shareholders in the event of a takeover. Baytree made a final offer of $473 million before finally withdrawing. For the second time in its history, Carson's had avoided an unwanted takeover.

While Carson's was busy buying and selling various business units, a company named P.A. Bergner was following a similar path. Bergner's was a regional department store chain that traced its roots to Peoria, right across the street from the original Block & Kuhl store that had been acquired by Carson's in the 1960s. Peter Alan Bergner built the six-story red brick store in 1889, and it remained in his family until 1938, when it was purchased by a Swiss company named Maus Frères. The store continued to operate as a single location until 1957, when a second store was built in Peoria's Sheridan Village Shopping Center. The new store was the largest in the state outside Chicago and reportedly had the highest sales volume per square foot of any

Carson's top executives—*left to right*, John T. Pirie Jr., Norbert F. Armour and C. Virgil Martin—attend a shareholders' meeting.

department store in the entire United States. After that success, the company quickly expanded across the region, and in 1985, it acquired all the Boston Store locations in Wisconsin, along with three Gimbels stores. Bergner's maintained the Boston Store identity in that state and simply operated under both banners. Bergner's was growing rapidly and was heading for its biggest acquisition yet.

In 1989, Bergner's made a bid to buy Carson Pirie Scott and Company. This was no corporate raider—this was a highly respected and experienced department store operator, and it had Carson's full attention. Bergner's wanted badly to break into larger markets such as Chicago and saw the chain as its ticket. After some negotiations, Bergner agreed to pay $343 million for the company and also took on $300 million of Carson's debt. The stores would continue to operate under the Carson Pirie Scott and Company nameplate. But although it seemed like a match made in heaven, the reality was much more dismal.

In truth, Bergner's had seriously overextended itself in its eagerness to close the deal. Its management had hoped to immediately spin off Carson's catalogue division to raise some quick capital, but it actually sold for much less than it had expected. Debts were mounting, and banks were reluctant to offer more credit to the now-struggling company. Maus Frères, Bergner's Swiss parent, reluctantly handed over $150 million as a short-term solution, but it was a case of "too little, too late." Sales had dropped as unpaid vendors halted shipments and the in-store inventories grew thin. Just two short years after buying Carson's, Bergner's was forced to file for bankruptcy protection. Fortunately, both the bankruptcy court and Bergner's creditors agreed that the company's business plan was sound; its troubles were due to the sudden untenable debt load, not from ongoing management lapses or lack of business. In fact, sales were beginning to rebound nicely. As part of its court-approved reorganization plan, the company was taken over by Dickstein Partners, a New York investment firm. Bergner's successfully emerged from bankruptcy in 1993 and assumed the corporate name of Carson Pirie Scott and Company.

The new company now operated fifty-nine stores in four midwestern states—Illinois, Indiana, Minnesota and Wisconsin. Finally back on solid ground, Carson's renewed its efforts to expand. It immediately set its sights on Younkers, an Iowa-based retailer that owned fifty-three stores covering seven states from Michigan to South Dakota. Younkers had recently emerged from its own bankruptcy and had no desire to change ownership again, so it rebuffed the initial offer of $152 million. Carson's persisted, and the battle turned ugly. After various legal maneuvers by both parties and more than a year of protracted court battles, Younkers successfully deflected the takeover bid in 1995, only to agree to a friendly merger with Proffitt's Inc. of Tennessee less than a year later. And almost before the dust had settled, Proffitt's made another acquisition: none other than Carson Pirie Scott and Company. The deal was finalized in 1998 for a value of $790 million. The stores continued to operate under their original names, but Proffitt's hadn't finished its buying spree; that same year, it acquired luxury retailer Saks Fifth Avenue and changed the corporate name to Saks Incorporated.

By now, the management and employees at Carson's probably needed to keep a running spreadsheet to determine who their corporate owner was on any given day, but most of the changes were relatively invisible to customers. Business continued at a steady pace even as the company structure continued to morph. In 2001, Carson's sold the State Street building to developer Joseph Freed and leased back the property. The unexpected deal was likely due to the fact that the aging structure was soon going to need major renovation, and it was a bill that Carson's did not want to incur. But there were many more changes down the road for the company in what would be the most significant decade in its more-than-150-year history.

Above: Carson's Great Artist's windows, like this one featuring Botticelli painting the Madonna, were exquisitely detailed.

Left: Detail from a Great Artist's window.

The 1974 Housewares Expo focused on home fashions and the latest kitchenware.

Chicago's busiest intersection was also home to Carson Pirie Scott for more than one hundred years. *Photo by Peter Rimsa.*

In 2006, Saks Incorporated sold the Carson Pirie Scott, Bergner's, Boston Store, Herberger's and Younkers names to Bon-Ton Stores for a reported $1.1 billion. Bon-Ton is a Pennsylvania-based department store chain, and the acquisition brought it to a total of 275 stores spanning twenty-three states from the Northeast to the Midwest and the Great Plains. The company describes itself as "not too big, not too small, but just right!" Its corporate philosophy embraces the diversity of its retail nameplates and pledges the following: "We'll continue our rich tradition of commitment to our individual communities and local store names. We'll be nimble and adapt to the ever-changing retail industry. We'll embrace new ideas, innovative creativity and differing points of view."

Briefly, it seemed that Carson Pirie Scott was on a healthy trajectory, but as it turned out, the end was near for the iconic State Street flagship store. Its landlord, Joseph Freed, hired Harboe Architects to undertake the project of restoring the landmark building. It soon became clear that the extensive renovation would be costly and lengthy. There was no practical way to operate a department store while the work was being performed, so Carson's would have to temporarily relocate. Freed, however, had a vision of turning the fully restored building into a more profitable mixed-use building. He was willing to lease back to Carson's, but at a price; ultimately, it was more than corporate parent Bon-Ton could stomach. So sadly, on February 21, 2007, Carson Pirie Scott and Company turned out the lights for the last time in the building that had been inextricably linked with its history for more than one hundred years.

The final tally for the restoration clocked in at about $190 million, but the result is an architectural gem for the city of Chicago. The once tired-looking building is now fresh and vibrant, and its ornamentation, which was worn and damaged and often replaced in a piecemeal fashion over the decades, now matches the original splendor of Sullivan's vision. The first two floors now house a flagship City Target, the discounter's model of a more upscale, sleeker version of its sprawling suburban stores. The seventh floor is home to the School of the Art Institute and the Sullivan Galleries. Other tenants include M. Arthur Gensler Jr. & Associates, a global architectural firm; Flat Top Grill; and a Carhartt clothing store. In 2012, Freed restructured the debt on the building but was forced to give up control of the property to a lending joint venture led by a Boston-based real estate investment trust.

State Street has changed considerably over the years. Once home to more than a dozen major department stores, it is now mostly occupied by discount retailers, cafés and small specialty shops. Of the original

The completely restored Sullivan Building now houses a City Target, among other tenants. *Photo by Peter Rimsa.*

department stores, only Sears remains. Wieboldt's, Montgomery Ward, The Fair, Mandel Brothers, Goldblatt's and most of the others have long since disappeared from the retail landscape. Marshall Field and Company closed in 2006 after its acquisition by Federated Department Stores, the corporate parent of Macy's, which now occupies the location. The Field's building was granted status as a National Historic Landmark in 1978, and in 2005, the City of Chicago also bestowed landmark status on it in an effort to protect it from significant changes under new ownership. The brass plaques on the side of the building still read "Marshall Field and Company," but the trademark green awnings are gone, replaced by black ones bearing the Macy's name.

Over the years, many of the commercial buildings have been torn down or repurposed for residential use. The new urban dwellers are typically more interested in smaller-scale practical businesses that supply daily necessities such as food and clothing or entertainment and dining opportunities; the massive old department stores catered to a crowd that had more leisure time and perhaps more patience. Why spend hours searching for an item when, with just a few clicks of a mouse, it can be delivered to your door? Department stores do still have their place but seem to be most successful when grouped in an environment that is conducive to "retail therapy," aka recreational shopping. In Chicago, that role has largely shifted from State Street to Michigan Avenue, the new street of merchants.

Carson Pirie Scott, now going by the single name "Carson's," is rumored to be considering a return to downtown someday, but for now the chain exists in mostly suburban locations. Bon-Ton, its corporate owner, was badly battered in the recent economic recession, along with most of the department store sector, but it hasn't given up the fight to grow and expand. In September 2013, it opened a new 122,000-square-foot store in Fort Wayne, Indiana, under the Carson's banner and received quite a warm welcome in the town. The company recently outlined its strategy in a filing with the Federal Securities and Exchange Commission (SEC). It characterized its target demographic as women, ages twenty-five to sixty, with average household incomes of $55,000 to $125,000 per year. Like the original Carson's management, Bon-Ton straddles the line between mid-income and upscale. Its new stores reflect its expected audience's needs, and the merchandise selection heavily favors women's apparel, shoes, purses, jewelry, cosmetics and accessories. It still carries menswear, household goods such as dishes and small appliances and bed and bath items, but the selection has been trimmed to focus on its core customer.

Under Bon-Ton's ownership, Carson's is continuing its long legacy of civic and community involvement. For many years, one of its most popular promotions has been its frequent Goodwill days, when customers who bring in a donation of clothing or outerwear in good condition will receive an immediate discount on their purchases. The collected items are sent to Goodwill Industries in support of its charitable work. Carson's has also been a longtime supporter of National Public Radio (NPR) and other cultural institutions. And in each market where they're located, the individual stores will work in concert with local nonprofits, allowing them to generate funding through the sale of Carson's coupon booklets.

There are some people who will proclaim that department stores are obsolete, a quaint throwback to the days of horse cars and buggy whips, and have no place in the fast-paced world of online commerce. But for the department stores that are able to withstand the capricious nature of the American economy and are willing to respond to consumers in a flexible and creative way, there will always be a niche. As the well-worn saying goes, "Everything old is new again," and that certainly applies to the retail sector. There's been a slow but steady march back to customer-centric, service-oriented businesses. For example, some grocery chains are dumping their once-heralded self-service checkouts after realizing that many shoppers found them to be annoying and difficult. But perhaps the truth went somewhat deeper than that; the self-service trend broke that very vital human connection that can make or break a store. Savvy retailers have learned that a warm smile and helpful attitude go a long way toward convincing a customer to buy a product or service. Price alone is no longer incentive enough for many people. The simple luxury of a pleasant shopping experience is often worth a few more pennies. That's the simple secret that kept Carson's in business for more than 150 years, and it's the key to its future.

In an old personnel manual that was left behind when the company moved away from State Street, there's one page that stood out among the rest. In bold letters, it read: "A *Chicago Tribune* survey established our 'image' as that of a 'friendly store' in the eyes of Chicagoland's people. This image is a priceless asset, and it should be our constant intention to preserve it and enhance it."

I don't think John Pirie or Sam Carson could have said it any better.

Chapter 9

CARSON'S CELEBRITY WALK OF FAME

On State Street, that great street, I just wanna say,
They do things they don't do on Broadway,
You'll have the time, the time of your life.
—"Chicago" lyrics by Fred Fisher

C hicago is a friendly town that welcomes all visitors, famous or not, and in many ways the two elegant department stores that once stood proudly on State Street—Carson Pirie Scott and Company and Marshall Field and Company—served as ambassadors for the city. They represented its culture, its people, its architecture and its aspirations. Perhaps due to the proximity of the iconic Palmer House Hotel, Carson's became a frequent stopping point for celebrities staying at the landmark inn. Palmer House's Golden Empire Dining Room offered entertainment and hosted legendary performers such as Frank Sinatra, Judy Garland, Ella Fitzgerald, Harry Belafonte, Louis Armstrong and, as they jokingly called him, "a little known pianist named Liberace." Whether they were in town to perform, promote a book or a movie or just passing through, many of these luminaries dropped by the store to greet customers and have a few publicity photos taken.

Carson's kept a large ornate French writing desk on the third floor in front of the rotunda windows for such occasions. Thus ensconced, the celebrity could hold court as adoring fans lined up to catch a glimpse or request an autograph. Afterward, Carson's would mount the glossy photo in a modest silver frame and hang it on the wall in the eighth-floor hallway leading to the store's auditorium. Over the years, it accrued quite a collection, and generations of children headed to see Santa Claus clearly recall the long walk down the "hall of fame." The following pages capture just a few of these memorable folks.

TONY CURTIS

Curtis, who was born as Bernard Schwartz in Bronx, New York, in 1925, was an American actor with more than one hundred films to his credit. In a career that spanned six decades, he displayed an amazing versatility, starring in roles that ranged from slapstick comedy to intense dramas. Some of his most notable films include *The Defiant Ones* (1958), *Some Like It Hot* (1959), *Sex and the Single Girl* (1964) and *The Boston Strangler* (1968). In later years, he made frequent television appearances. Curtis was also a prolific and talented surrealist painter, with some of his works appraised at more than $25,000. In his later years, he

focused primarily on his art, leaving Hollywood behind.

Tony married his first wife, actress Janet Leigh, in 1951, but they divorced in 1962. He went on to marry five more times. His many marriages produced six children, among them actress Jamie Lee Curtis.

Curtis died at his home in Henderson, Nevada, on September 29, 2010.

Tony Curtis waves hello to Chicagoans from a replica of San Francisco's famous cable car.

Phyllis Diller

Diller was born Phyllis Ada Driver in Lima, Ohio, in 1917. She began her career in radio but soon advanced to stand-up comedy. Eventually, she worked her way into television and film, including appearances with Bob Hope during the 1960s. She accompanied Hope to Vietnam in 1966 with his USO troupe during the height of the Vietnam War and later credited him for much of her success. Diller cultivated a stage persona that was wacky, outspoken and self-deprecating. She was known for her wild hair and clothes, along with her frequent discussions of the various plastic surgery procedures she had undergone.

Her first marriage to Sherwood Anderson Diller produced six children but eventually ended in divorce. She then married actor Warde Donovan, although the union lasted just three months. Diller continued entertaining until her ninetieth birthday, when health issues finally put an end to her career.

She passed away on August 20, 2012, in her Los Angeles home at the age of ninety-five, with "a smile on her face," according to her family.

Phyllis Diller mugs for the camera in front of Carson Pirie Scott's famed rotunda entrance.

MAYOR AND MRS. DALEY

Richard J. Daley served as mayor of Chicago for twenty-one years and was chairman of the Cook County Democratic Central Committee for twenty-three years, holding both positions until his death in office in 1976. Daley was born in 1902 in the working-class Chicago neighborhood of Bridgeport, and he remained there his entire life. In 1936, he married Eleanor "Sis" Guilfoyle. They had seven children, three of whom followed their father into politics. Their youngest son, William, served as the secretary of commerce under President Bill Clinton and later served as White House chief of staff under President Barack Obama. Richard M. Daley, the oldest son, was elected mayor of Chicago in 1989 and served in that position until his retirement in 2011. Son John is a member of the Cook County Board of Commissioners.

The senior Daley achieved worldwide notoriety during the 1968 Democratic National Convention in Chicago, when antiwar protesters clashed with police and National Guardsmen in what was later termed a "police riot." Images of the bloody confrontation were captured on news feeds and spread around the globe.

Mayor Richard J. Daley (center) and his wife with executives from Carson Pirie Scott.

On December 20, 1976, Daley suffered a massive heart attack while visiting his doctor and died at the age of seventy-four.

CHARLTON HESTON

Actor Charlton Heston was born John Charles Carter in 1923 in an unincorporated section of Wilmette, Illinois. He starred in more than one hundred films over the course of his career, including *The Ten Commandments* (1956), *Ben-Hur* (1959), *El Cid* (1961) and *Planet of the Apes* (1968). His performance in *Ben Hur* garnered him an Oscar for Best Actor.

In 1944, Heston enlisted in the army, but not before he married a Northwestern University student named Lydia Marie Clarke, a union that produced one son. After his return from active duty, he and his wife moved to New York City, where he earned roles on Broadway and in television before making it to Hollywood and the silver screen.

Heston was known as much for his political activism as for his acting. Originally a liberal Democrat, he slowly transitioned over the years to a staunch neoconservative. Eventually, he established his own political action fundraising committee and became deeply involved with the National Rifle Association.

On April 5, 2008, Heston passed away from pneumonia at

Charlton Heston signs autographs in Carson's auditorium.

his home in Beverly Hills, California, with Lydia, his wife of sixty-four years, by his side.

C. VIRGIL MARTIN AND PRINCE PHILIP OF ENGLAND

Prince Philip, the Duke of Edinburgh, is the husband of Queen Elizabeth II and holds the distinction of being the oldest and the longest-serving spouse of a reigning British monarch. He was born into a Greek and Danish royal family in 1921 and was titled "Prince Philip of Greece and Denmark," but the family was exiled when he was still a child. In 1947, he married Princess Elizabeth, his third cousin and presumptive heiress to the monarchy. The couple had four children: Prince Charles, Princess Anne, Prince Andrew and Prince Edward.

In February 1952, King George VI—Elizabeth's father—died, and she ascended to the throne.

Prince Philip (right) is welcomed to Carson's by CEO C. Virgil Martin.

Socialite Charlotte Ford gives a talk at Carson's. Charlotte is an American automotive heiress and socialite, the daughter of Henry Ford II. She was born in 1941, and in 1966, she married Stavros Spyros Niarchos, a Greek shipping tycoon, who was thirty-two years her senior. Their daughter, Elena Anne Ford, was born later that year. Niarchos and Ford divorced a year later, and Ford turned her focus to various charities, including the Police Athletic League (PAL).

Polly Bergen and Lee Phillips at Carson's. Polly Bergen, who was born Nellie Paulina Burgin in 1930, is an American actress, singer, television host and entrepreneur. Some of her films include *Cape Fear* (1962), *The Caretakers* (1963) and *Murder on Flight 502* (1975). Lee Phillips was born in 1928 and is a former talk show host and soap opera creator. She was executive producer of *The Bold and the Beautiful* and *The Young and the Restless*.

Marlo Thomas speaks to the crowd at Carson's. Marlo Thomas was born on November 21, 1937, as Margaret Julia Thomas to comedian Danny Thomas and his wife, Rose Marie Cassaniti. Marlo is an American actress, producer and social activist best known for her role on the television series *That Girl*. She is married to talk show host Phil Donohue, and she also serves as national outreach director for St. Jude Children's Research Hospital. In her brilliant career, Thomas has received four Emmy Awards, a Golden Globe Award, a Grammy Award, a Jefferson Award and the George Foster Peabody Award.

Helen Hayes signs autographs in Carson's bookstore. Hayes was born in 1900 in Washington, D.C. She was known as the "First Lady of the American Theater" for her career, which spanned seventy years. Helen is one of only eleven people who have won an Emmy, a Grammy, an Oscar and a Tony Award. She was an active philanthropist, and in 1983, Hayes received the award for Greatest Public Service Benefiting the Disadvantaged from the Jefferson Awards.

Mayor Jane Byrne and her husband, journalist Jay McMullen, at Carson's. Jane Margaret Byrne was born on May 24, 1934, in Chicago and became its first (and only) female mayor. She served from April 16, 1979, to April 29, 1983, when she was narrowly defeated for reelection by Harold Washington, Chicago's first (and only) African American mayor. Byrne has one daughter, Kathy, and a grandchild. Recent health problems have kept her out of the spotlight.

Wally Phillips greets customers at Carson's bookshop. Phillips was born on July 7, 1925, in Portsmouth, Ohio. He came to Chicago in 1956 and hosted WGN's morning radio show for twenty-one years, from January 1965 until July 1986; he was number one in the morning slot. His show was one of the first to use prank phone calls and other humorous skits on the air. He was also a philanthropist, and in 1969, he founded the Neediest Kids Fund, which has since raised $35 million for charity. In 2004, the street corner of Rush Street and Delaware Street in Chicago was designated as Honorary Wally Phillips Way.

About the Author

Gayle Soucek is an author and freelance editor with more than a dozen books to her credit, including *Marshall Field's: The Store That Helped Build Chicago*; *Chicago Calamities: Disaster in the Windy City*; and a few other titles with The History Press. She is a lifelong Chicagoan and Blackhawks hockey fan, residing in the far northwest suburbs with her photographer husband, dogs, parrots, reptiles and one very laid-back cat. History, architecture and shopping—not necessarily in that order—are her favorite Chicago pastimes, and she relished the opportunity to revisit State Street in these pages.

Visit us at
www.historypress.net
···
This title is also available as an e-book